Should Teens Have Access to Birth Control?

Don Nardo

INCONTROVERSY

ReferencePoint
Press®

San Diego, CA

© 2014 ReferencePoint Press, Inc.
Printed in the United States

For more information, contact:
ReferencePoint Press, Inc.
PO Box 27779
San Diego, CA 92198
www.ReferencePointPress.com

LIBRARY OF CONGRESS CATALOGING-IN-PUBLICATION DATA

Nardo, Don, 1947–
    Should teens have access to birth control? / by Don Nardo.
       p. cm. -- (In controversy)
    Includes bibliographical references and index.
       ISBN 978-1-60152-556-7 (hardback) -- ISBN 1-60152-556-7 (hardback)
    1. Birth control--United States--Juvenile literature. 2. Teenagers--Sexual behavior--Juvenile literature. 3. Sex instruction for teenagers--United States--Juvenile literature. 4. Contraceptives--United States--Juvenile literature. 5. Sexual abstinence--United States--Juvenile literature. I. Title.
    HQ766.8.N37   2013
    306.708350973--dc23
                                                                              2012043607

Contents

Foreword

In 2008, as the US economy and economies worldwide were falling into the worst recession since the Great Depression, most Americans had difficulty comprehending the complexity, magnitude, and scope of what was happening. As is often the case with a complex, controversial issue such as this historic global economic recession, looking at the problem as a whole can be overwhelming and often does not lead to understanding. One way to better comprehend such a large issue or event is to break it into smaller parts. The intricacies of global economic recession may be difficult to understand, but one can gain insight by instead beginning with an individual contributing factor, such as the real estate market. When examined through a narrower lens, complex issues become clearer and easier to evaluate.

This is the idea behind ReferencePoint Press's *In Controversy* series. The series examines the complex, controversial issues of the day by breaking them into smaller pieces. Rather than looking at the stem cell research debate as a whole, a title would examine an important aspect of the debate such as *Is Stem Cell Research Necessary?* or *Is Embryonic Stem Cell Research Ethical?* By studying the central issues of the debate individually, researchers gain a more solid and focused understanding of the topic as a whole.

Each book in the series provides a clear, insightful discussion of the issues, integrating facts and a variety of contrasting opinions for a solid, balanced perspective. Personal accounts and direct quotes from academic and professional experts, advocacy groups, politicians, and others enhance the narrative. Sidebars add depth to the discussion by expanding on important ideas and events. For quick reference, a list of key facts concludes every chapter. Source notes, an annotated organizations list, bibliography, and index provide student researchers with additional tools for papers and class discussion.

The *In Controversy* series also challenges students to think critically about issues, to improve their problem-solving skills, and to sharpen their ability to form educated opinions. As President Barack Obama stated in a March 2009 speech, success in the twenty-first century will not be measurable merely by students' ability to "fill in a bubble on a test but whether they possess 21st century skills like problem-solving and critical thinking and entrepreneurship and creativity." Those who possess these skills will have a strong foundation for whatever lies ahead.

No one can know for certain what sort of world awaits today's students. What we can assume, however, is that those who are inquisitive about a wide range of issues; open-minded to divergent views; aware of bias and opinion; and able to reason, reflect, and reconsider will be best prepared for the future. As the international development organization Oxfam notes, "Today's young people will grow up to be the citizens of the future: but what that future holds for them is uncertain. We can be quite confident, however, that they will be faced with decisions about a wide range of issues on which people have differing, contradictory views. If they are to develop as global citizens all young people should have the opportunity to engage with these controversial issues."

In Controversy helps today's students better prepare for tomorrow. An understanding of the complex issues that drive our world and the ability to think critically about them are essential components of contributing, competing, and succeeding in the twenty-first century.

Differing Approaches to a Real Crisis

A seventeen-year-old high school senior who asked to be called Heidi recently expressed a great deal of dismay about her and her classmates' lack of access to birth control information and devices. Her school did not offer these things to students. Also, most of the young people Heidi knew were too fearful or embarrassed to approach their parents or doctors and ask for help with contraception.

What disturbed Heidi the most about this situation was that a fair number of students at her school were having sex, and of those who were, many of the young women were getting pregnant. "Currently we have 5 girls pregnant at our school," Heidi stated with a touch of alarm. "And since I was a freshman there has been a total of 27 girls who have become pregnant. Also, there are 6 girls from last year's senior class who just found out they were pregnant a month after graduation. I think it is ridiculous and messed up how many girls think it's cute that they are pregnant."[1]

Heidi attributed this high number of pregnancies to the girls' and their boyfriends' failure to use contraception. She went on to say that her school offered a sex education class for seniors. But it lasted only three days, which was far too short, in her view. The teacher spent most of the three days describing the various diseases someone could

> *"I think it is ridiculous and messed up how many girls think it's cute that they are pregnant."*[1]
>
> — Heidi, a high school student.

catch from having sex, an approach clearly intended to scare the students into refraining from becoming sexually active. The teacher made no attempt to describe the diverse birth control methods and devices available that might keep the young women from getting pregnant.

"I think schools aren't taking it serious," Heidi exclaimed. "They should have part of the blame because kids spend 75% of their time at school." However, she added, parents bear some blame, too, for the ongoing rash of teen pregnancies at the school.

> Parents need to talk to their children and tell them, "look, this is what will happen," and they need to be serious. I think parents these days are trying to be more of friends than actual parents. I think every girl who is thinking about becoming sexually active or who is already sexually active needs to be on birth control. [The government] needs to make a law where girls can go and get birth control without a parent because I think a lot of children and parents don't talk because of the embarrassment.[2]

Statistics Raise Concerns

Many American parents, medical professionals, and government and social organizations agree with Heidi that teen pregnancy happens too frequently in the United States. They also agree that the main reason this is happening is that some teens, for various reasons, have unprotected sex. Unprotected sex is best defined as having sexual intercourse without using a contraceptive, or birth control, device.

Statistics confirm that the concerns expressed by Heidi and the others are fully warranted. Large numbers of American teenagers are indeed having sex, and many of them do not use birth control of any kind. According to the Guttmacher Institute, a national organization that works toward the advancement of sexual and reproductive health, about half of teens aged fifteen to nineteen have had sex at least once. Also, approximately 750,000 of the young women in this group get pregnant every year. Moreover, the Guttmacher researchers found, 82 percent of those pregnancies are neither expected nor planned in advance. In part this is because teens who have sex on a regular basis but do not use birth control have a 90 percent chance of getting pregnant in any given year.

Most of the teenage women who get pregnant unintentionally pay some sort of unwanted price. "Having a child during the teen years carries high costs—emotionally, physically, and financially—to the mother, father, child, and community,"[3] says a spokesperson for Project Cap, a division of Planned Parenthood, the country's biggest reproductive health–care provider. Among these costs are the incidence of miscarriage and abortion, both of which can put a physical and emotional strain on the young women who undergo them. Roughly 14 percent of the teens who unexpectedly get pregnant each year have miscarriages, and about 29 percent of them choose abortion.

Most of these teen abortions occur because the young women who have them are "concerned about the ability to care for the baby financially, emotionally and physically,"[4] the Guttmacher Institute points out. Indeed, the fact that most teens are not yet mentally or emotionally ready to become strong, effective parents is one of the leading arguments for giving teens access to birth control.

How Society Is Affected

Whether or not one agrees that granting such access is wise, virtually everyone concurs that unplanned teen pregnancies often have detrimental effects on society. Many pregnant teens drop out of high school and fail to get a diploma, for example. In fact, only about half of teenage mothers go on to earn a high school diploma by age twenty-two. In stark contrast, fully 90 percent of teenage girls who do *not* get pregnant and have a child *do* graduate high school by the time they are twenty-two. Furthermore, because they lack a diploma, the young women in the first group have a much more difficult time finding good jobs when they are in their twenties and thirties.

Teenage girls who get pregnant also pass along high costs to US taxpayers. Many of these young women, along with their families, cannot afford to pay for prenatal care, the necessary medi-

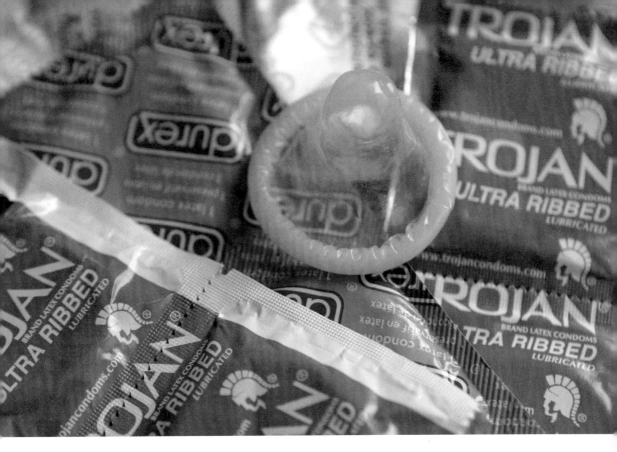

cal attention a woman receives while pregnant. Nor can they pay the hospital costs for giving birth to their children. In many cases those costs are absorbed by the state and federal governments, which are funded by taxpayer dollars. As a result, unplanned teen pregnancies cost the American public roughly $9 billion each year.

Moreover, it is widely acknowledged that if not addressed and remedied, these problems can continue to plague the nation later. Studies have shown that the daughters of teenage parents are nearly 33 percent more likely to become pregnant when they themselves are teens. In this way an ongoing and seemingly unending cycle of teen pregnancy can result.

A Moral and Political Quagmire

For these reasons, unwanted teen pregnancies constitute a costly problem each year in physical, emotional, medical, and financial costs alike. Some Americans argue that allowing teens regular access to birth control will greatly reduce these costs. By using con-

Although many forms of birth control are available, and some—such as condoms—are relatively easy to buy, statistics show that many teens who are sexually active do not use contraceptives of any kind.

traception responsibly, they say, teens will avoid unplanned pregnancy and the many harmful consequences it frequently produces.

In contrast, others insist that it would be more ethical and effective to try to decrease the incidence of teens having sex. Obviously, they say, if most young people did not engage in sexual activities, both teen pregnancy and teens' need for birth control would be nearly eliminated. Those who think this way advocate such approaches as teaching students to abstain completely from sex and requiring that parents be notified if their teenagers seek to use birth control.

People on different sides of the issue clearly do not see eye to eye. The topic of teen access to birth control and its consequences "is often a moral and political quagmire,"[5] say journalists Edward Sztukowski and Lynn Schwebach. Arguments on both sides are loud and sometimes even angry. But in the long run, some sort of compromise will have to be worked out. The fact is, Sztukowski and Schwebach say, "a real crisis is occurring in America beyond politics, war, or religion—a crisis that affects the development of life skills, setting of goals, and financial stability of America's teenagers."[6] All involved can agree that this crisis—the existence of large numbers of unwanted pregnancies each year—must be dealt with sooner or later.

Facts

- According to the Centers for Disease Control and Prevention (CDC), during the past twenty years, the rate of teen girls having children has dropped by about 40 percent, but approximately eleven hundred teen girls still give birth every day.

- According to the Guttmacher Institute, black women aged fifteen to nineteen have the highest rate of teen pregnancy in the United States, followed by Hispanics and then Caucasians.

CHAPTER ONE

How Did the Availability of Birth Control to Teens Become Controversial?

The question of why so many American teenagers have unprotected sex resulting in teen pregnancy has plagued parents,
educators, legislators, medical authorities, and concerned citizens alike in recent decades. "When birth control is so available,"
writes Kathleen London of the Yale–New Haven Teachers Institute, "why do so many adolescents continue to become pregnant?
And of course the answer is not easy." She explains:

> Birth control failure is high for adolescents and commit-
> ment to effective use is often lacking. You may wish to
> consider the following points: no method is 100% effec-
> tive; health care providers may not take time to fully edu-
> cate clients; the commitment to use contraception effec-
> tively may be lacking because the young woman and man
> are not comfortable with their sexuality, are experiencing
> guilt or shame about being sexually active, have not fully
> examined their feelings about the person with whom they

are having intercourse, and may not have a feeling of personal control in the relationship. In addition, birth control services have not been consistently and appropriately available to teenagers.[7]

London recognizes that the availability of birth control literature and devices for teens is highly controversial. Some people think it is proper to give teenagers access to birth control through schools, clinics, individual doctors, or other means. Other Americans hold that granting such access is improper because, among other things, it can effectively give teens the green light to experiment with sex. Moreover, some people view teens having sex, whether using contraception or not, as morally wrong.

This difference of opinion should not and cannot be debated in a vacuum, London believes. One way that teens, their parents, health-care professionals, and legislators can all come to understand the issue better, she says, is by examining where both the issue and the controversy came from. That necessitates a brief look into the past, especially the years directly preceding and during the sexual revolution of the 1960s, to see how prior generations dealt with the birth control issue. "An examination of the folklore and politics of birth control" in the mid-twentieth century, London states, "and of how the issues, pro and con, have been politically negotiated over the years" may encourage young people, parents, and others "to reflect on their own attitudes and the origins of them." Thereby, she adds, they may well come "to re-evaluate them."[8]

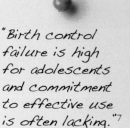

"Birth control failure is high for adolescents and commitment to effective use is often lacking."[7]

— Kathleen London, Yale–New Haven Teachers Institute.

Two Major Advances

Neither the existence of teen pregnancy nor the use of birth control are new phenomena. In many prior eras and societies, it was fully expected that teenagers would have sex and that teenage girls would get pregnant. This was because the age at which people married and had children was much younger than it is today. Also, contraceptive methods of various kinds have been used throughout recorded history, although until the mid- to

The Challenge of Changing Behavior

During World War I, which started in 1914, the US military made a large-scale attempt to change the sexual behavior of thousands of American soldiers. Some of America's allies in the conflict became worried when large numbers of their soldiers and sailors came down with gonorrhea and other sexually transmitted diseases, or STDs. So they began issuing these fighters condoms, which were known to provide fairly good protection against these ailments.

In contrast, US military officials tried a different approach—ordering the men to refrain from having sex while stationed overseas. That way, hopefully, they would not catch any STDs and issuing condoms would be unnecessary. Only about 30 percent of US military personnel obeyed the order. However, large numbers of US soldiers did not contract STDs, primarily because they obtained condoms while abroad.

late nineteenth century, most were moderately effective at best.

The first major modern advance in birth control was an outgrowth of the vulcanization of rubber in 1839. It allowed a large-scale industry that produced fairly reliable condoms to develop in the United States. Rubber condoms, which aptly came to be called "rubbers" for short, steadily became the most popular type of contraceptive in the United States, Europe, and elsewhere.

The second major advance in contraception, one that made the 1960s sexual revolution possible, was the emergence of the birth control pill. "The pill," as it is frequently called, grew out of the efforts of some of the early figures of the women's movement in the United States. Among these highly influential feminists, who were also strong birth control advocates, were Emma Goldman and Margaret Sanger. It was Sanger who in 1914 actually coined the term *birth control*. Writing for the Daily Beast, journalist Johannah Cornblatt states:

Born to an Irish-Catholic family, Sanger watched her mother, worn out after 18 pregnancies and 11 live births, die slowly. In a series of articles titled "What Every Girl Should Know" and in her newspaper, *The Woman Rebel*, Sanger strived to provide women with information about contraception. At neighborhood clinics, she provided women with controlled forms of birth control. Sanger is perhaps most well known for founding the American Birth Control League, which eventually became Planned Parenthood, in 1921.[9]

Sanger and other major feminists of the early 1900s urged women to use birth control in order to help them and their husbands plan the size of their families. All people—women and men alike, and young, unmarried people as well—should have access to safe, efficient birth control, these feminists insisted. This conviction was based on the notion that each person, whether male or female, should have the innate right to have control over his or her own body.

Development of the Pill

As the women's movement continued to gain strength in the decades that followed, Sanger and others continued to fight for women's right to plan the size of their families. They should also be able to rely on a safe, effective form of birth control that did not depend on men, Sanger said. In other words, the condom had its advantages. But in any relationship the man both supplied and used it, giving him the ultimate power over the woman's safety and frequently her future.

Feminists like Sanger called for the creation of a completely new kind of birth control—some sort of contraceptive that would both prevent pregnancy and be totally under a woman's personal control. The problem was that inventing and mass-producing such a product was an extremely expensive and time-consuming undertaking. For a long time no person or organization with the required wealth came forward to accept the challenge.

Finally, in the early 1950s the aging Sanger persuaded the rich

American feminist, biologist, and philanthropist Katherine Mc-Cormick to enter the fray. McCormick's equally wealthy husband, Cyrus McCormick, was diagnosed with schizophrenia, a mental disorder characterized by various thought and behavioral problems. Worried that the condition might be genetic, or inherited, she decided she would never get pregnant and have children. None of the contraceptive methods then in use prevented pregnancy effectively enough, in her view. So she poured enormous sums of money into research on a new, more protective form of birth control.

The eventual result of these exhaustive studies and tests was the biggest turning point in the modern history of contraception—the birth control pill. Typically, it contains the hormones estrogen and progesterone. When taken once a day for a set number of days each month, it keeps a woman from ovulating, or releasing an egg

Margaret Sanger was at the forefront of efforts in the early 1900s to develop a safe and effective method of contraception. The result of those efforts was the development of the birth control pill.

into her uterus. If male sperm cells that enter her reproductive tract find no egg to fertilize, no pregnancy can occur. Fulfilling the hopes and dreams of Sanger and other feminists, the pill has proved to be 99.9 percent effective if used properly.

Legal Status

The first birth control pill, called Envoid, hit the market in 1957. Pending further tests, the US Food and Drug Administration (FDA) approved it only for treating menstrual disorders, or problems with a woman's monthly period. This was partly because the pill was effective in helping alleviate such disorders. More importantly, however, it was because selling or otherwise supplying contraceptives was still against the law in thirty states. Even in Massachusetts, which was in many ways more socially liberal than most other states, selling birth control devices was a crime in 1957. If caught and convicted, a person could be sentenced to five years in prison.

After conducting some studies, however, in 1960 the FDA approved the pill for its primary purpose, preventing pregnancy. A mere three years later, it was already the most popular contraceptive in the Western world. Nevertheless, in the United States it was legally available only in those states where selling contraceptives was allowed. That finally changed in 1965. The Supreme Court's decision in the case of *Griswold v. Connecticut* made buying birth control devices a matter of personal privacy and thereby legal everywhere in the country. (This was for married people only. Contraceptives did not become legal for unmarried people until the 1970s.)

Opening Up Dangerous Possibilities?

There was another reason the pill was initially approved in 1957 only to treat menstrual disorders. Namely, people in positions of power, including the FDA, other government agencies, and most doctors, feared the advent of a widespread change in sexual mores. So they proceeded slowly and carefully with the pill in what they hoped would be a conservative, safe manner. As Gary F. Kelly, author of *America's Sexual Transformation*, explains:

Suddenly, physicians were writing prescriptions for the ovulation-blocking medicine under the guise of treating [menstrual] discomforts. The government and the American Medical Association seemed to be colluding [working together] at a more formal level to keep a lid on American sexual desire, for once the pill was approved as a method of birth control in 1960, it could still be prescribed only as such for *married* women.[10]

Contraceptives and the Right to Privacy

In the now famous case *Griswold v. Connecticut*, the Supreme Court handed down a ruling that led the way to making birth control legal across the United States. Alex McBride, an editor for the *Tulane Law Review*, provides this concise snapshot of the case's background and the reasoning of a majority of the justices.

> Estelle Griswold, the executive director of the Planned Parenthood League of Connecticut, and Dr. C. Lee Buxton, doctor and professor at Yale Medical School, were arrested and found guilty as accessories to providing illegal contraception. They were fined $100 each. Griswold and Buxton appealed to the Supreme Court of Errors of Connecticut, claiming that the law violated the U.S. Constitution. The Connecticut court upheld the conviction, and Griswold and Buxton appealed to the U.S. Supreme Court, which reviewed the case in 1965. The Supreme Court, in a 7–2 decision written by Justice William O. Douglas, ruled that the law violated the "right to marital privacy" and could not be enforced against married people.

Alex McBride, "*Griswold v. Connecticut* (1965)," PBS, December 2006. www.pbs.org.

For those married women who did start using the pill, and their husbands, the pill seemed like a godsend. It allowed couples to plan and control the size of their families with a very minimal chance of failure and unintended pregnancy. Also, women could finally feel like they were in control of their reproductive organs and at least to some degree their own futures.

Not everyone was happy about this new contraceptive advance, however. Another crucial consequence of the pill's arrival was its potential illegal use by unmarried teenagers. Some Americans—particularly devoutly religious individuals and political conservatives—worried that teens and other young people would get access to it and use it in an irresponsible manner. One common fear was that young people would abandon traditional morals and lapse into an orgy of sexual promiscuity.

In 1966, for example, John Alexander, general director of the Inter-Varsity Christian Fellowship, headquartered in Chicago, said: "I think it is certain that the pill will tear down the barriers for more than a few young people hitherto restrained by fear of pregnancy."[11] Equal alarm over the coming of the pill was voiced by Richard S. Emrich, former bishop of the Episcopal Diocese of Michigan. "The existence of the pill opens up dangerous possibilities," he stated. "It provides an invitation to premarital sex. There must be limitations and restrictions on the use of sex if we are to remain a civilized people."[12] Several state health departments were also alarmed. Connecticut's chief health officials estimated that one out of every six thirteen-year-old girls in the state would become pregnant without getting married before they reached age twenty.

From Conformity to Individualism

That prediction never came true. Yet the pill did end up causing extensive and far-reaching changes in the way Americans viewed and practiced sex. Historians generally concur that to a large degree the pill made the sexual revolution of the 1960s possible. That upheaval in sexuality was part of a much larger set of social changes often referred to as the 1960s cultural revolution. In both cases the term *1960s* is something of a misnomer. The cultural and sexual revolutions did not get going in earnest until around 1964 or so; the cultural revolution lasted well into the mid-1970s; and most historians feel that the sexual revolution continued into the early 1980s.

In whatever manner one chooses to date these megatrends, they wrought enormous changes in American society. In their wake, many Americans rebelled against what they considered to be old-fashioned social rules and traditions, gender discrimination, and an unjust war in Vietnam. A counterculture, or movement against the traditional cultural norms, developed, as historian John C. McWilliams explains. "Hippies, or young people distressed with mainstream society, challenged widely accepted social practices and espoused an alternative lifestyle." As a result, he says, "traditional conformity gave way to unprecedented individualism and a reexamination of the conventional code of conduct. Change is inevitable and seldom a graceful operation, but the cultural revolution it produced in the 1960s was as profound as it was pervasive, touching virtually every aspect of American life."[13]

Partly because the cultural revolution was so pervasive, or widespread, as McWilliams says, transformations in one cultural area influenced those in several others. For example, the pill had provided the initial impetus for changes in sexual behavior. Yet other cultural factors inspired some people to be bolder and more radical about such behavior. Opposition to the Vietnam War, for instance, caused many young people to question the values and policies of the country's leaders and more generally the status quo. So did the civil rights movement that demanded that African Americans be accorded the same rights and treatment as the white majority.

Efforts to end the war and bring about racial equality reflected the view of members of the growing counterculture that certain social ideals of prior generations had been wrongheaded and needed to be changed. Similarly, these same young people increasingly voiced the notion that their parents and grandparents had been sexually repressed. Or at least, the general argument went, their natural sexual expression had been stifled by a society that was too rigid, prudish, and militaristic. "Make love, not war" became the

> "The existence of the pill opens up dangerous possibilities. It provides an invitation to premarital sex."[12]
>
> — Richard S. Emrich, former bishop of the Episcopal Diocese of Michigan.

counterculture's proverbial call for instigating a new age characterized by sexual freedom and peace among the nations.

Driving the Revolution Forward

More and more invigorated by the expanding cultural revolution, the leaders of the sexual revolution grew ever more daring in voicing their beliefs and demands for substantive change. The means they employed included public demonstrations; publication of books, magazines, newspaper articles, and pamphlets; use of more explicit lyrics in songs; and increased nudity and sexually charged situations and language in stage plays and films. Among the movies that overtly exploited sexual themes and did well at the box office were *I Am Curious (Yellow)*, *Blow-Up*, and *Midnight Cowboy*. (In 1970 *Midnight Cowboy*, which had been released the year before, became the first X-rated film to win the Academy Award for

Best Picture.) Meanwhile, Broadway plays that reflected "the new openness," McWilliams points out, "included *Hair*, billed as 'an American tribal love-rock musical' and featuring nudity and four-letter words. *Oh! Calcutta* was a popular nude review [small-scale musical]. Each production enjoyed more than a thousand performances on and off Broadway. The older generation wrung its hands over a supposed collapse of morality."[14]

Although the mostly male playwrights and filmmakers who created these movies and plays did help drive the sexual revolution forward, they could not match the efforts of growing numbers of smart, talented, and intrepid women. Armed with birth control pills and other contraceptives, as historian Nancy L. Cohen says, they were "the true warriors" of the movement. They were

> young, single women, who, with the help of this new contraception, took their sexuality into their own hands. If not for women's self-determined sexual liberation, the sexual revolution might have been another unremarkable episode in the long and varied sexual history of humankind. Instead, with the impetus the sexual revolution gave to a new feminism and a movement for gay liberation, it became one of the major catalysts of America's ongoing political delirium [frenzy].[15]

One of the leading feminists in this group was Helen Gurley Brown, who published a highly provocative book titled *Sex and the Single Girl* in 1962. In an article for the popular magazine *Atlantic*, social and religious critic R. Albert Mohler Jr. tells why the book ignited a firestorm of controversy:

> Helen Gurley Brown dared to scandalize the nation, virtually inventing the "single girl" as a cultural category. Brown urged young women to see themselves as empowered by sex, money, and men—but without any need for the traditional commitment to marriage. Her argument was so scandalous at the time that no major publisher would

"If not for women's self-determined sexual liberation, the sexual revolution might have been another unremarkable episode in the long and varied sexual history of humankind."[15]

— Historian Nancy L. Cohen.

touch the book. The bookstores were filled with books offering advice to young wives and mothers, but Helen Gurley Brown was openly inventing a new cultural category, the sexually liberated single girl. The single girl "is engaging because she lives by her wits," declared Brown, who pointed to her younger self as a prime example of the empowered single girl she now celebrated. And, most central to Brown's vision, the single girl is having sex, a lot of sex, and enjoying romantic relations with men, lots of men.[16]

The Floodgates of Worry

Brown and other leading feminists insisted that women must have access to birth control. The pill was central to women's efforts to control their own bodies and avoid pregnancy when they so chose. But an increasing number of other methods became available over the years. A popular one was the diaphragm, a dome-shaped rubber shield. A woman places it inside her vagina, covering the cervix, so that no male sperm can get through the cervix and into the uterus. Also popular were spermicides—liquids, creams, or jellies applied to the vaginal area to inhibit the potency of male sperm and thereby prevent pregnancy.

Over time, increasingly widespread use of the pill, condoms, diaphragms, spermicides, and other kinds of birth control had a dramatic effect on American sexual practices. The sexual activities and overall lives of women, including teenage women, were particularly affected by the sexual revolution. Indeed, "the rapidity of change in women's sexual behavior was dizzying," Cohen states.

> In the 1950s, six in ten women were virgins at marriage and 87 percent of American women believed that it was wrong for a woman to engage in premarital sex, even with "a man she is going to marry." By the time girls born during the sexual revolution came of age, the double standard—in practice, if not exactly in the minds of teenage boys—had been obliterated. Only two in ten of them would be virgins at marriage. Teenagers, in particular, shed the old ways. In 1960, half of unmarried 19-year-old women had

not yet had sex. In the late 1980s, half of all American girls engaged in sexual intercourse by the age of 17, two-thirds by the age of 18, and the difference between teenage male and female sexual experience had narrowed.[17]

Statistics like these opened the proverbial floodgates of worry by some parents, pastors, teachers, and legislators about teen access to birth control. Their general attitude was that teens should not be able to easily acquire the pill, condoms, or other contraceptives because this would encourage them to have sex. In contrast, large numbers of people came to see these fears as groundless. They became convinced that access to birth control does not make teens more likely to have sex. At present, there appears to be no end in sight to the ongoing debate between these two decidedly opinionated and passionate groups.

Facts

- By their nineteenth birthday, seven in ten American female and male teens have had intercourse, the CDC reports.

- According to the Guttmacher Institute, 10 percent of all US births are to girls aged nineteen or younger.

- Nearly one in five (19 percent) female teens at risk for unintended pregnancy were not using any contraceptive method at last intercourse, the Guttmacher Institute says.

- According to the National Center for Health Statistics, the condom is the most common contraceptive method used by teens at first intercourse.

- The National Campaign to Prevent Teen Pregnancy says that 82 percent of teen pregnancies are unplanned; also, teens account for about one-fifth of all unintended pregnancies annually.

Should Schools Make Birth Control Available to Teens?

Each succeeding year witnesses renewed debate in the United States about whether or not schools should be allowed to dispense birth control to students who request it. In 2010 T.C. Williams High School in Alexandria, Virginia, became part of that debate. It opened a health center for teens in the school building next door to the guidance office. For more than twenty years, the clinic, which during the 2010 opening received a new name—the Teen Wellness Center—had been located three blocks away from the school.

School officials cited two main reasons for moving the clinic, which is run by a full-time primary care doctor and a licensed nurse practitioner. First, it was hoped that more students would avail themselves of the general health services the center had long offered, such as first aid, sports physicals, and substance abuse counseling. A majority of the students in the school district are from low-income families, many of which lack health insurance. So, as one of the school's teachers, Patrick Welsh, explained, a free clinic within the school "can deal with health issues that might otherwise go untreated or cost taxpayers thousands of dollars in emergency room care."[18]

The second reason for reopening the clinic inside the school was far more controversial. In the prior few years, its staff had also dispensed birth control information and devices, including condoms, to students aged twelve to nineteen. When the health center was *separate* from the school, approximately fifty female students got pregnant each year. That amounted to one in every twenty girls. School department officials were optimistic that if the center was situated *inside* the high school, more teens might use it to acquire contraceptives. In turn, that might bring down the yearly pregnancy rate among adolescents in the district.

Pro and Con

The policy of allowing the health center to hand out contraceptives inside T.C. Williams High School caused a great deal of discussion and debate in the two years following its implementation. Opinions, both pro and con, came from students, parents, and members of the larger community, including local health-care professionals and religious leaders. Newspaper, radio, and television editorials from around the state, as well as from neighboring states, also weighed in.

Much of the opposition to distribution of contraceptives by the school clinic was based on the worry that this approach might encourage young people to have sex. Typical of those who made this argument was a local priest, Dennis Kleinmann. He stated that giving the students free condoms and other contraceptives offered them an easy way to avoid the risks of pregnancy. In turn, in a very real sense that gave them the green light to go ahead and indulge in sexual activity. "Our position would be that they shouldn't be having sex," Kleinmann said, "and that if you are handing these out you are encouraging it."[19]

Supporters of the new high school contraceptive policy disagreed with this argument. They said that if giving the students free birth control made them more sexually active, there would likely have been an increase in teen pregnancies during the two years fol-

Condom displays such as this are found in many pharmacies and other stores around the country. There are no age restrictions on condom purchases, but many sexually active teens are too embarrassed to buy them.

lowing the startup of the health center. The reality, the supporters pointed out, was that the number of yearly student pregnancies actually decreased from fifty to twenty during that period.

Reasons for Supplying Birth Control

The Alexandria school system's ongoing experiment with providing teenagers with birth control represents a single example of many similar trials occurring across the United States. The exact number of public schools that make condoms or other contraceptives available to their students is uncertain and constantly changing. The last year in which relevant data was reported in this regard was 2011. At that time the CDC estimated that close to five hundred US public schools gave students access to birth control. This number represented a little more than 1 percent of middle schools and a bit more than 5 percent of high schools.

As a rule, the school systems involved cite more or less the same reasons that Alexandria does for instituting this still-controversial policy. First, they hope that regular use of contraceptives will reduce the number of teen pregnancies that occur each year. As an added bonus, they expect the decrease in teen pregnancies to help reduce the incidence of teenagers having abortions. Also, giving teens access to birth control will supposedly promote a sense of responsibility and self-discipline among them.

Still another reason for supplying birth control in schools, according to advocates of these programs, is to fill a gap in health-care services that exists in many US communities. Making sure that teens have access to contraceptives, the advocates say, is key to reducing unwanted pregnancies among teens. The problem, they point out, is that nonschool sources do not by themselves reach enough young people. Some teens, for instance, get contraceptives through their parents. Other teens buy condoms at local pharmacies, as there is no age requirement to purchase condoms. A majority of young people avoid this route, however. Their reasons vary; some are embarrassed to ask for birth control, or they may be afraid the pharmacist will tell their parents. Others may mistakenly assume that someone has to be eighteen to buy contraceptives, and still others may not be able to afford it.

The birth control pill, meanwhile, requires a prescription from a doctor or nurse practitioner. The prescriptions are available from those family doctors who feel comfortable providing them, as well as from private health-care centers and clinics run by organizations like Planned Parenthood. But for their own reasons, only some of the teens who are sexually active use these sources to obtain the pill.

In marked contrast, studies show that reaching students in their school settings is a significantly easier and more effective way to make sure they receive and use birth control. Providing condoms at school health centers is a good example. According to the University of Wisconsin Population Health Institute, "School-based condom availability programs appear to increase condom acquisition among adolescents and may also increase condom use."[20] Based on this evidence, therefore, pro-access advocates feel their overall goal—to reduce teen pregnancies—is well served by distributing condoms in schools.

> "School-based condom availability programs appear to increase condom acquisition among adolescents and may also increase condom use."[20]
>
> — University of Wisconsin Population Health Institute.

The School Clinic's Mission

In 2010 the new Teen Wellness Center made its debut at T.C. Williams High School in Alexandria, Virginia. The center defined its mission, saying in part:

> The new location of the Teen Wellness Center facilitates stronger collaborations among City departments, organizations, and community partners. Through this transformation and re-location, the Center will increase opportunities for health education and make services more accessible and available to even more Alexandrian teens. The Teen Wellness Center provides a variety of health services to youth between the ages of 12–19 years. These services include treatment of minor illnesses, immunizations, and physical examinations required for schools, participation in sports, employment, and the Special Olympics. Written parental consent is required before any of the aforementioned services can be provided.
>
> In addition, the Teen Wellness Center provides health education, behavior change counseling, pregnancy testing, diagnosis and treatment of sexually transmitted diseases, reproductive health services (to include the provision of birth control methods), and mental health and substance abuse counseling. State law permits these services to be offered without parental consent.

Quoted in City of Alexandria, Virginia, "The Teen Wellness Center," June 29, 2012. http://alexandriava.gov.

General Reactions

Reactions from students to these contraceptive distribution policies have been almost uniformly positive. Most of the schools that have instituted such policies have had roughly the same experience that Alexandria's T.C. Williams High School had. During the new Teen Wellness Center's first two years of operation, student use of the facility nearly doubled. The number of young people asking for and receiving contraceptives increased significantly (although there was no immediate way to tell how many actually used them).

In general, community reactions to new school clinics of this kind have also closely resembled those in Alexandria. There, after an initial period of intense discussion and debate, the controversy died down and the clinic became more or less accepted. Some members of the community still disapproved of the policy of giving teens free access to contraceptives. But no one mounted a major effort to change or discontinue the policy.

This pattern has been repeated time and again across the country, going back at least as far as the early 1990s. In 1991, for example, Falmouth became the second Massachusetts town to begin distributing contraceptives in a school-based health clinic. Initially, the Falmouth school district's daring move was a hot topic of conversation and debate in the town, in neighboring communities, and across the state. "We were the first school in the state to put condom vending machines in bathrooms," former Falmouth school superintendent Robert Antonucci stated in 2010. Arguments were "very heated," he recalled. "I can remember being chastised at Mass by a local priest."[21] A number of parents also initially objected to the new policy, and a group of them filed a suit against the school district. But the effort failed when the Massachusetts Supreme Court ruled in favor of the school district in 1995.

Room for Growth and Expansion?

After that, no more significant objections to the Falmouth school program surfaced. Moreover, in the years that followed, similar clinics that dispensed contraceptives to students appeared in other schools in Massachusetts. According to the *Boston Globe*, more than two dozen of the state's school districts now have such programs. They include Bedford, Provincetown, Newton, Revere, and Boston. (Eight of Boston's forty-odd high schools provide condoms, and in some cases other forms of contraception, to students.)

This increase in school-based contraception distribution programs was not limited to Massachusetts. Rather, it was part of the growing trend that brought the number of participating schools to roughly five hundred by 2011. In addition, in 2012, school districts in Brooklyn, New York; Springfield, Massachusetts; and New London, Connecticut; instituted such programs.

Hundreds of other school systems nationwide have begun to debate whether or not to start their own versions of these programs. Although there is no way to predict how many will actually do so, experts indicate there is plenty of room for growth. The National Assembly on School-Based Health Care estimates that somewhat more than two thousand school-based health clinics currently exist. Of these, about a quarter, located in more than four hundred school districts, dispense contraceptives to students. The Center for Education Reform in Washington, DC, estimates there are about 13,800 school districts in the United States. That means that only about one in every thirty-four districts currently has such a program, leaving enormous potential for expansion in the future.

The Question of Increased Sexual Activity

Irrespective of their numbers, however, both the need for and legitimacy of such programs is far from settled. As more and more schools have instituted clinics that give students free birth control, certain issues and concerns continue to be voiced by those who oppose this policy. In response, advocates of the policy regularly try to counter the opponents' arguments with their own, and so the national debate over giving teens access to contraceptives in schools persists.

A major concern is that dispensing birth control to students in schools might encourage young people who were not previously sexually active to start experimenting with sex; it might also encourage students who are already sexually active to have sex more often. According to Greg Pfundstein, executive director of the Chiaroscuro Foundation, a pro-life advocacy group, this happens because of a phenomenon known as risk compensation. It consists of people acting in a *less* cautious manner when they perceive that a situation is safe and behaving *more* cautiously when they feel the situation is less safe. Thus, Pfundstein suggests, when teens have free access to birth control, they will assume they are fully protected against pregnancy. That makes them overconfident, which in turn induces them to become sexually active or in some cases, *more* sexually active.

As more young people have sex, Pfundstein says, the likelihood of mistakes in contraceptive use will also grow. "Access to contraception and abortion alters the sex and mating markets," he explains,

"The fear that making condoms available will increase sexual activity, a primary political obstacle to making condoms available to high school students, appears to be unfounded."[23]

— Health-care expert Sally Guttmacher.

and, through risk compensation, actually increases the number of unintended pregnancies. Just as anti-lock brakes lead drivers to drive faster, follow closer, and brake later, the already nearly universal access to contraception seems to increase the number of sexual encounters, thereby increasing the number of contraceptive failures. We know risk compensation is at work with bicycle helmets, seatbelts, ski helmets, and skydiving gear. To deny its obvious role in the sex and mating markets is to let ideology triumph over reason and science.[22]

Advocates of distributing contraceptives in schools disagree with this analysis and maintain that this policy does not cause young people to feel freer to engage in sex. To support this assertion, the advocates cite a study conducted by New York University public health expert Sally Guttmacher and several of her colleagues. These experts compared New York City public high schools that have clinics that dispense birth control to almost identical public high schools in Chicago. The only significant difference was that the Chicago schools do not dispense contraceptives to their students. The study found that rates of sexual activity were roughly the same in both sets of schools. "Thus," Guttmacher and the others stated in their report, "the fear that making condoms

A mother and daughter discuss the use of birth control pills. Many Americans feel strongly that it is the role of parents, not schools, to discuss sexuality with their children and to be involved in decisions relating to contraception.

available will increase sexual activity, a primary political obstacle to making condoms available to high school students, appears to be unfounded."[23]

Opponents acknowledge the results of the Guttmacher study. But they caution that it surveyed only two school districts out of many hundreds. So the study's findings may well be anecdotal, or based on one or a few isolated instances and therefore unreliable.

Usurping Parents' Roles?

Another concern that opponents of the policy often raise is that when schools provide teens with birth control, they usurp a role that should be played by the students' parents. Schools and parents have certain separate responsibilities regarding young people, the opponents say. One of the jobs traditionally assumed by parents is educating their children about sexuality, including contraception. "School staff often seems to forget that the children they see every day are not their own," says health researcher and mother Rebecca

Mikulin. "Their job is to educate kids. End of story. This does not mean teaching moral issues or 'life issues.'" She adds, "If the students want contraceptives, it is not the school's responsibility to give it to them, nor should they. A student needs to be mature enough to discuss the issue with his or her parents."[24]

Advocates of the policy say that leaving instruction about sexuality strictly to parents *would* be preferable. But it would work effectively only in a perfect world. In the real world, the advocates argue, some parents are absent from the home, and even among those who *are* home, many do not feel comfortable talking to their children about sexuality or contraception.

Additionally, some parents lack the expertise to give competent advice about birth control. Former high school biology teacher and school therapist Rosemary Redfern points out that dispensing contraceptives to teens should be accompanied by "expert advice on how to use it, and what the consequences are if they don't. Not all children have adults they can talk to or relate to and the peculiar ideas children develop about sex through misinformation are surprising."[25]

The Arrival of Plan B

Concerns have also surfaced on the subject of which types of contraceptives school programs choose to give students. Condoms are the most common form of birth control distributed in schools, followed by birth control pills. Other contraceptives provided by some high school clinics include injections, patches, and rings—and all have supporters and detractors. But the type of contraception that raises the loudest opposition is Plan B, otherwise known as the "morning-after pill" or "emergency contraception." Plan B consists of hormones—frequently, though not always, the same ones found in regular birth control pills, only in considerably higher or more concentrated doses. Emergency contraception disrupts fertilization and/or ovulation inside a woman's reproductive tract. (The initial step in any pregnancy, fertilization, or conception, occurs when a male's sperm unites with a female's egg. Ovulation is

"School staff often seems to forget that the children they see every day are not their own. Their job is to educate kids. End of story."[24]

— Health researcher Rebecca Mikulin.

33

the process in which an egg is released by one of a woman's ovaries. If ovulation is disrupted, no egg reaches the reproductive tract to meet up with any sperm that may be present.)

What makes the morning-after pill so controversial is reflected in its very nickname. A woman takes it soon *after* she has sex, a fact that has caused opponents of school-based birth control clinics to condemn it. In their view, it encourages teenagers to have as much sex as they want and not even worry about using condoms or other standard kinds of contraception. In such cases any worries about pregnancy could be eliminated simply by resorting to Plan B.

New York City Schools and Plan B

So far, it appears that the only school system that has dispensed the morning-after pill is New York City's. (The National Association of School Nurses states that it is unaware of any other school district that distributes Plan B.) New York City made front page news in 2011 and 2012 when its school district significantly expanded a little-known test program involving Plan B. Almost overnight, the city began giving out morning-after pills to female students as young as fourteen in several of its public high schools.

City health officials claimed they were responding in the most aggressive and effective way possible to a virtual epidemic of teen pregnancies in the school system. More than seven thousand young women aged fifteen to seventeen had been getting pregnant each year in New York City. Moreover, some two-thirds of those girls chose to end their pregnancies by having abortions, and seven out of ten of them dropped out of school. The new birth control program was an attempt to drastically reduce both teen pregnancies and abortions, as well as keep more young girls in school, the officials explained.

Reactions by opponents of the city's emergency contraception program were swift and highly critical. Valerie Huber, president of the National Abstinence Education Association in Washington, DC, called it "a terrible case once again of bigotry of low expectations."[26] By this, she meant that many people assume that teens are going to have sex no matter what. So people should stop trying to dissuade them from it and just cater to their whims. Mean-

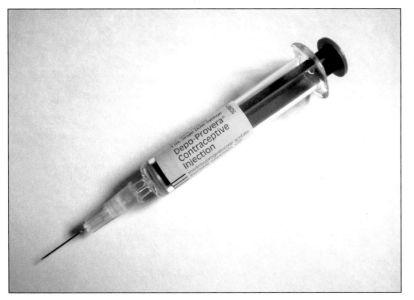

Health clinics at some US high schools provide contraceptives of various types to students who request them. Depo Provera, a contraceptive hormone injection (pictured), is offered at some of these clinics.

while, a prominent group that opposes distributing birth control in schools weighed in. The New York City Parents' Choice Coalition claimed that the ongoing implementation of Plan B would "change teen behavior in a way that will result in an increase in sexually transmitted diseases."[27]

Although the complaints about dispensing Plan B were many and loud, some New Yorkers vigorously defended the program. The city's mayor, Michael Bloomberg, argued that pregnancies among students were so numerous that other forms of birth control were by themselves not enough to deal with the problem. So resorting to the morning-after pill was a necessity. "The good news," he stated, "is we've brought teenage pregnancy down by, I think, something like 25 percent over the last 10 years. The bad news is there's still an awful lot of girls who get pregnant at a very early age."[28]

Among several medical experts who back Bloomberg's advocacy of giving Plan B to students is Cora Breuner, a member of an American Academy of Pediatrics committee on teen health. She maintains that the morning-after pill is safe and effective "if you use it in a timely fashion. It provides relief or solace to a young woman or man who has made a mistake but doesn't want to have to live with that mistake for the rest of their lives."[29]

Opposed to New York City's Plan B

In 2012 a group of antiaccess advocates called the New York City Parents' Choice Coalition released an open letter to the city's mayor, Michael Bloomberg, and to the director of the city's public school system. The coalition was highly critical of the system's recent distribution of Plan B contraception. The letter read in part:

> We would prefer an informed consent program that requires an affirmative "opt-in" by parents and respects their personal beliefs.
>
> Furthermore, no one questions the idea that giving teens access to Plan B will work to decrease teenage pregnancies. But we should question it, because there is no evidence that it will, and in fact there is some evidence that the increased access will change teen behavior in a way that will result in an increase in sexually transmitted diseases.

New York City Parents' Choice Coalition. "Open Letter to Mayor Bloomberg and Chancellor Walcott." www.nycparentschoice.org.

The Debate Goes On

Whether or not other US school systems will follow New York's lead in dispensing Plan B remains to be seen. Breuner and a number of her colleagues believe that other schools *should* begin providing the morning-after pill if they feel that other birth control methods are not working well enough.

Rich Lowry, editor of the influential *National Review*, takes a very different position. In fact, he not only thinks that schools should not give students Plan B, he also opposes giving them the pill and other forms of contraception. Summing up the general opposition to such policies, he writes:

If easy, widespread access to contraception were the answer to teenage pregnancy, the New York schools would have solved the problem long ago. More access to the latest contraceptive technology isn't going to make a difference. It is true that the schools can't substitute for the discipline and values that kids aren't getting at home. But they shouldn't be the friend and the enabler of the sexually active teenager, either.[30]

Some US schools have been providing students birth control of one form or another for more than two decades. None of these schools closed down their contraceptive distribution programs because of public opposition. So although heartfelt disagreement still exists, it is unlikely that any of the existing programs will be terminated in the near future.

Facts

- **The Georgia Campaign for Adolescent Pregnancy Prevention reports that each year, almost 750,000 US women aged fifteen to nineteen become pregnant.**

- **Only about 5 percent of American high schools make condoms available to students, the Guttmacher Institute says.**

- **According to the Pew Forum, 78 percent of American parents want public schools to teach about birth control.**

- **The majority of sexually experienced teens (78 percent of females and 85 percent of males) used contraceptives the first time they had sex, a Child Trends Research Brief indicates.**

Should Parental Consent Be Required for Teens Who Want Birth Control?

The debate over teens' access to birth control has generated a number of divisive side issues. One of the most controversial is whether or not a young person who seeks to obtain contraceptives should first be required to get a parent's consent. That issue came to the fore with particular urgency and spawned unprecedented expressions of parental outrage in 2011. This was when the New York City Department of Education made national headlines by expanding its experimental program that dispenses Plan B contraception to students.

Both supporters and opponents of the program recognized that the education department's actions ignited two major, and often separate, arguments. One was over whether schools should distribute birth control. The other focused on the issue of parental consent, which is not always confined to school settings.

In the case of the New York schools and Plan B, many parents, as well as numerous conservative organizations, were quick to take offense and convey their anger. They were indignant that the school department had not alerted and consulted with the parents before launching the program. In their view, the decision to give students, including some in their early teens, a contraceptive as potent and controversial as Plan B should not be made by city and school personnel on their own. Rather, parents should be included in the decision process. Moreover, they should have the right to keep their children from participating in the program if they so choose.

Opt Out or Opt In?

School department officials just as quickly pointed out that they had sent "opt-out" letters home with every student in August 2011. The letters informed parents about the city's intent to dispense the morning-after pill, along with other contraceptives, the officials said. Furthermore, the words "I DO NOT want my child to receive the following services"[31] appeared at the bottom, alongside a space for the signature of a parent or guardian. By signing, that person ensured that his or her child would be excluded from the program.

This was not enough for the program's opponents, however. The New York City Parents' Choice Coalition summed up the opposition's objection, saying, "While we agree with the goal of reducing unwanted pregnancies, we object to the deceptive means employed by the Department of Education to disengage parents from important, potentially life-altering health care decisions involving their minor children."[32]

What the coalition found deceptive was the school department's selection of an opt-out, as opposed to an opt-in, approach. As Rich Lowry puts it, "Parents have to explicitly choose to 'opt out' of the program, which, as any behavioral economist will tell you, strongly tips the balance toward its passive acceptance."[33] In other words, in an opt-out approach, it is understood that all students will take part in the program unless a parent specifically forbids his or her child from participating. The problem, Lowry and others point out, is that expecting hundreds of thousands of parents all to respond to a

"While we agree with the goal of reducing unwanted pregnancies, we object to the deceptive means employed by the Department of Education to disengage parents from important, potentially life-altering health care decisions involving their minor children."[32]

— New York City Parents' Choice Coalition.

letter sent home with students is unrealistic. In addition to those parents who read the letter but are too busy to respond, many others may never even see it. "Are the parents really informed, I wonder?" asks Joyce Slaton. "We certainly manage to miss papers from our daughter's school. There's always a blizzard of forms and flyers and notices. Do the papers come in an envelope, in the mail, all on their own? Or are they stuck in the kids' homework folders, where a harried parent might easily miss them?"[34]

This might explain why only a little more than 1 percent of New York City parents signed and submitted opt-out letters for the new birth control program, says Mona Davids, president of the New York City Parents Union. That volunteer group, which opposes the program, holds that an opt-in permission slip would be fairer and more efficient for parents. "When your daughter has gone on a [school field] trip, didn't you have to sign that it's OK for her to go on a trip?"[35] Davids asks. With such an approach, she says, the only participants in the program would be the students whose parents specifically approved.

Privacy a Fundamental Right

Defenders of the program and the opt-out approach to parental notification disagree with these arguments. They assert that in matters of health care, parental rights are frequently superseded, or outweighed, by young people's right to privacy. In fact, they point out, New York is one of twenty-five states (along with the District of Columbia) that give minors the legal authority to consent to contraceptive services on their own, without parental consent. Thus, supporters of the policy say, the act of notifying parents about the school's new program is a courtesy, not a parental right.

Those supporters go further by calling on parents to recognize that all human beings, including teens, have a right to privacy, especially in sexual matters. They add that obtaining contraceptives clearly falls under the heading of sexual matters. That position is well articulated by the Center for Reproductive Rights, an American organization that views reproductive freedom as a fundamental human right that all governments should protect, respect, and

fulfill. "Access to contraceptive services," the center states, "is considered a fundamental privacy right and has remained so for over three decades."[36] An article in the medical journal *Perspectives on Sexual and Reproductive Health* elaborates, saying:

> Youth-serving agencies and medical professionals recognize the important roles that parents play in the lives of adolescents. However, many also believe that confidential access to sexual health services is essential for adolescents who are, or are about to become, sexually active because some teenagers might avoid seeking contraceptive and STD services if they were forced to involve their parents.[37]

The Same Protections as Adults

These arguments between New York City school officials and local parents over the Plan B distribution program exemplify a much larger debate and battle that is occurring nationwide. It pits an

Some New York City parents were angered to learn that the Plan B contraceptive was being offered without parental consent to students in some of the city's public schools. Plan B, displayed here by a pharmacist, is commonly known as the morning-after pill because it is taken shortly after sexual intercourse.

unknown number of young people against an equally uncertain number of parents. The young people in question desire to acquire contraceptives. Meanwhile, the parents insist that minors should have to obtain parental permission first.

The events in New York City are not the only instance in which parents who feel this way have encountered a veritable wall of frustration. For more than three decades, US teens have been allowed to obtain contraceptives without parental consent. This has been possible whether they get them from a school, private clinic, doctor, Internet site, or other source.

To date, none of the fifty states specifically requires parental consent or notification for minors who want to acquire birth control. That legal state of affairs stems in large part from the 1977 US Supreme Court case *Carey v. Population Services International*. In a 7–2 vote, the justices declared that it was unconstitutional to ban the sale of birth control to minors. In delivering the majority opinion, Justice William Brennan held that minors are permitted the same constitutional protections as adults. Among these protections, he wrote, is the right to privacy. It includes the right of a person, whether married or single, an adult or a minor, to be free of society's or the government's attempts to control his or her decisions relating to intimate, or sexual, relations.

As a result of this ruling, therefore, American teens enjoy complete confidentiality when they receive contraceptives from a school, private clinic, doctor, or other source. To the aggravation of many parents, this gives young people an extraordinary degree of reproductive freedom. Not all adolescents are aware of the high court's momentous 1977 decision. Like many parents, they mistakenly assume that parents have the legal right to decide whether or not minors can have access to birth control. So an unknown number of teens do not seek to obtain contraceptives because they think their parents will forbid it.

Texas Enacts Limits

To the relief of many parents, however, their lack of legal authority to control their children's attempts to acquire contraceptives is by no means settled. State and federal lawmakers have wrestled with

The Controversial Opt-Out Letter

The opt-out letter from the New York City Department of Education to parents regarding its policy to provide Plan B, or emergency contraception, to students said in part:

> Services will be provided by a school nurse and a School Health doctor. The program will include: reproductive health counseling and education; referrals for additional care; pregnancy testing (urine testing, no physical exam required); emergency contraception (EC); birth control pills; condoms and social work services. Students must sign a form consenting to these services prior to receiving them. All services are confidential and free of charge. Under New York State law, minors may receive reproductive health services without parental consent. However, because this program will operate in a public school, you may inform us that you do not want your child (if under age 18) to receive birth control pills, EC (emergency contraception), condoms and/or pregnancy testing through this program by returning the bottom of this letter to the principal.

New York City Department of Health and Mental Hygiene, "CATCH Opt-Out Letter," New York City Parents' Choice Coalition, August 2011. www.nycparentschoice.org.

this issue for many years. Although their efforts have not always been successful, they continue to propose laws that would in one way or another get around the 1977 Supreme Court ruling.

On the state level, for example, in 1997 the Texas legislature tried to ban the use of any state money that might end up giving contraceptives to teens. A majority of the legislators voted to forbid using family planning funds to pay for prescription drugs intended for minors who had not gotten their parents' consent. Oral contraceptives like the birth control pill are prescription drugs. So this law would have kept teens from obtaining oral contraceptives unless their parents said it was all right.

Because some Texans disagreed with the proposed statute, it was soon reviewed by the Texas Supreme Court. The justices concluded that no one would be unduly harmed by the law. So they did not block it, and it went into effect in 1998. Most of the justices agreed that parental consent was appropriate in cases involving teens and contraceptives. In a statement they made in a ruling in a related case later in 1998, they stated:

> We trust that it is not out of date for the state and its courts to be concerned with the welfare of the family as the most vital unit in our society. We recognize that peace, tranquility and discipline in the home are endowed and inspired by higher authority than statutory enactments and court decisions. Harmonious family relationships depend on filial [child] and parental love and respect which can neither be created nor preserved by legislatures or courts. The most we can do is to prevent the judicial system from being used to disrupt the wide sphere of reasonable discretion which is necessary in order for parents to properly exercise their responsibility to provide nurture, care, and discipline for their children.[38]

As it turned out, however, the new rule did little or nothing to stop young people from acquiring birth control without parental consent. This was because the law banned the use of *state* funds that contributed to teens' access to contraceptives. A number of clinics in Texas continued to supply minors with birth control using *federal* monies, the use of which was not bound by getting parental consent. So those teens who wanted to obtain contraceptives simply went to federally funded clinics.

Similar Efforts Fail in Other States

Two years later, in 2000, the South Carolina legislature tried a somewhat different approach to force teens seeking contraceptives to get parental permission. A bill was proposed in the state

House of Representatives. It specifically targeted minors under age sixteen whose parents had requested that the state health department not give their children condoms and other kinds of contraceptives. The law's proponents sought to ban the use of state funds to provide birth control to young people in that category. The proponents managed to get the bill passed in the state House. But it failed to pass in the state Senate, so the law never went into effect.

Legislators in other states had been closely watching the South Carolina lawmakers' earnest efforts to formulate and pass the parental permission bill. When they saw it go down to defeat, it put a damper on similar efforts in those states. In state after state, the arguments put forth by lawmakers and others who opposed such bills carried the day. The Center for Reproductive Rights summed up several of these arguments, writing:

> These proposed laws threaten adolescent health and well-being. Even teens who could comply with parental consent requirements will face delays in getting contraceptive services. Additional clinic visits, missed school or work time, and increased expense will result. Many young women live in nontraditional situations—with one parent, a stepparent, other relatives, or on their own. Contact with biological parents, if required by law, may be impossible. Some teens face violence or other severe consequences from parents as a result of informing their parents that they are seeking contraceptive services. Minors fearful of retribution may forgo using contraception altogether, even though they are already sexually active.[39]

Efforts by Federal Lawmakers

Meanwhile, similar legislative efforts on the federal level were usually even less successful than those on the state level. Concerned parties who sought to stand up for parents' right to consent to their children's acquisition of contraceptives were largely unsuccessful.

"Some teens face violence or other severe consequences from parents as a result of informing their parents that they are seeking contraceptive services."[39]

— Center for Reproductive Rights.

One important reason for this outcome was the existence of Title X. Enacted in 1970, Title X is a federal program that mandates confidentiality for minors in cases in which they seek birth control.

Title X–supported health clinics encourage teens to consult with their parents when seeking contraceptive services from those clinics. But neither parental notification nor parental permission is legally required. So a young person can walk into such a clinic and obtain birth control without his or her parents' knowledge.

Over the years, conservative lawmakers in Congress have attempted to modify Title X by adding the condition that minors

Title X Defends Confidentiality

The federal program known as Title X upholds the policy of confidentiality and rejects parental notification in cases in which teens seek contraception. According to Planned Parenthood, Title X "has been key to helping millions of American women prevent unintended pregnancies and obtain reproductive health care for almost four decades." Defending Title X's support of confidentiality for teens, Planned Parenthood points out that

> research shows that confidentiality is crucial to teens' willingness to seek sensitive services such as family planning. Moreover, the fact that the average teen does not visit a family planning clinic until 14 months after she has become sexually active provides clear evidence that clinics do not encourage sexual activity. In fact, requiring parental consent will not discourage teens from having sex but will only deter them from seeking needed reproductive health care in a timely manner.

Planned Parenthood Action Center, "Title X: America's Family Planning Program," 2010. www.plannedparenthoodaction.org.

must get parental consent before they can receive contraceptive services in Title X–supported clinics. In 1998, for instance, the House of Representatives approved a requirement that young people who want birth control must first notify their parents. When the bill went before the Senate, however, it failed to pass, so the bill did not become law.

A similar legislative effort occurred a few years later. In 2005 Senator Tom Coburn, a conservative Republican from Oklahoma who is also a medical doctor, introduced a bill dubbed the Parents' Right to Know Act. He and his supporters hoped to produce a legal requirement that parents be notified when their teenagers try to acquire birth control. Replying to the initial criticisms of his efforts, Coburn said:

> This bill does nothing but put parents back in charge of their adolescent daughters. In almost every area of our children's lives, strict parental notification standards and laws are in place. For example, as a practicing physician, I am required to receive parental authorization, except in emergency situations, before I can provide any medical care to a child. Our schools require a permission slip from a parent before the school can give their child aspirin. Yet, at the same time, children can obtain prescription contraceptives at public health clinics without even notifying their parents.[40]

"Our schools require a permission slip from a parent before the school can give their child aspirin. Yet, at the same time, children can obtain prescription contraceptives at public health clinics without even notifying their parents."[40]

— US senator Tom Coburn.

Coburn's bill did not make it into law, however, partly because numerous doctors and health-care organizations lobbied against it. One of the groups that opposed it was the National Health Law Program, whose goal is to protect the health-care rights of low-income citizens. The group's summer 2005 newsletter claimed that Coburn's bill threatened the health of adolescents. It stated in part, "Studies have shown that requiring parental notification or consent for contraceptives for adolescents will not deter them from engaging in sexual activity. Rather they will simply delay or forego obtaining contraceptives and other medical treatment, placing their health and the health of their partners at risk."[41]

Immature Teens

No one on either side of the issue wants to put young people at risk. But a number of parents and others who advocate parental consent argue that teens need guidance in making crucial decisions, including whether to use contraceptives. One reason such guidance is necessary, some medical experts say, is that most teens are not yet emotionally mature enough to make such important choices on their own. In large part, according to this view, a teenager's brain is still developing. So he or she is really not in a position to make the best decisions about matters such as sex and birth control.

Among the experts who put forward this argument is Temple University psychologist Laurence Steinberg. "We need to rethink our whole approach to preventing teen risk," he states. "Adolescents are at an age where they do not have full capacity to control themselves. As adults, we need to do some of the controlling."[42] In cases of minors seeking birth control, Steinberg says, this controlling would take the form of parental consent.

Opponents of laws that would require parental consent in such cases do not deny that many minors are immature and prone to making decisions before thinking things through. Yet such personality flaws do not and should not override teens' right to privacy, those opponents insist. They point out that when the Supreme Court ruled in 1977 that a minor has a right to privacy, it did not mention his or her level of maturity or other disqualifying exceptions. One expert who agrees with this argument is noted Indiana University professor of education Annette Lamb. She admits that "research reveals that teens are immature and can make poor choices in social situations." Nevertheless, "teens have the right to privacy,"[43] a right that supersedes any personal limitations.

Tattoos, Pierced Ears, and Birth Control

Another frequently heard argument for forcing adolescents who want contraceptives to get parental consent compares birth control to other things that teens typically seek. For instance, many states have laws requiring minors to obtain a parent's permission to get a tattoo or to have their ears pierced—but not for getting birth control. As Coburn noted, schools cannot even give students

Many states require teenagers to obtain parental consent before they can get tattoos or pierced ears. This fact is frequently raised by parents who think they should also have a say-so in whether their teens have access to birth control.

aspirin without a parent's consent. According to this view, it makes no sense to demand parental permission to get aspirin but not to demand it to obtain birth control.

The Supreme Court's 1977 ruling is clear, however: In matters of personal relations, for both adults and minors, seeking contraceptives is protected by the right to privacy. Obtaining aspirin, tattoos, or pierced ears has no bearing on sexuality. Such acts are therefore *not* protected by the right to privacy, so parental permission can be and often is required.

Dialogue and Understanding

The contentious issue of parental consent is not likely to fade from the national or local debate over teen access to birth control. But open dialogue—between schools and parents and between parents and their teenagers—might lead to some form of compromise. Or at the very least, such a dialogue might lead to greater understanding of the strongly held views on all sides.

Facts

- According to a survey by the *Journal of the American Medical Association,* one in five teenage girls would not use birth control if they were required to notify their parents about seeking sexual health services.

- Girls who reside with their mothers or female guardians are more likely to tell the parent or guardian that they are seeking or using contraceptives than girls who live with their fathers, the *Journal of the American Medical Association* states.

- Planned Parenthood reports that 60 percent of teens who have visited a clinic to obtain contraceptives say that a parent or guardian sent them or knew they were there.

- Eighty percent of teenage girls whose parents know they regularly obtain birth control from a clinic or school say they will continue to use the clinic in the future, according to the *Journal of the American Medical Association.*

- The *Journal of the American Medical Association* says that 95 percent of female and male teenagers say they would continue to attend a clinic or see a doctor for STD counseling or treatment if parental notification became the law.

CHAPTER FOUR

Should Abstinence Be the Sole Birth Control Method Taught to Teens?

T he state of California banned abstinence-only sex education in its schools in 2003. No high schools or middle schools were supposed to teach abstinence-only after that. So two mothers with children in California schools were surprised and upset when they found that abstinence-only was still being taught there in 2012.

Abstinence means totally refraining from sex. In the context of modern discussions, it generally refers to young people waiting until they are married to begin having sexual relations. "Abstinence-only" is a catch phrase referring to an educational approach. In it schools stress abstinence as the only viable way to avoid pregnancy and do not teach about contraceptives or other methods, except to say that they do not work.

Turning to the Courts

The two mothers who discovered that this approach was still being taught are Aubree Smith and Mica Ghimenti. Both are residents of Clovis, a suburb of Fresno, in central California. They were aware that many California school systems had employed abstinence-only programs in their sex education classes up until 2003. In that year doctors and other local medical authorities had told California legislators that in their view evidence had shown that the abstinence-only approach was largely ineffective.

On the basis of this advice, the legislature revamped the state's basic approach to sex education. It passed a law stating that sex ed classes must present to students "medically accurate information on the methods of preventing pregnancy and sexually transmitted diseases (STDs)." Further, the law says, the teaching of sex ed "shall reflect the latest information and recommendation of the United States Surgeon General, the federal Centers for Disease Control and Prevention (CDC), and the National Academy of Sciences."[44]

Smith and Ghimenti also learned that the state Department of Education had on several occasions warned the Clovis Unified School District it was violating state law by using an abstinence-only program in its five high schools. Yet the district had ignored these warnings. This worried the mothers because they knew that since 2000 the Fresno region had had one of the highest rates of teen pregnancy in the state.

So in August 2012 Smith and Ghimenti sued the Clovis school system. They alleged that the district was endangering the health of students by continuing to pursue an abstinence-only approach to sex education. The American Academy of Pediatrics and the Gay-Straight Alliance Network joined them in the suit.

The Existing Program Unrealistic?

When the suit became public knowledge, local residents immediately took sides. So did other Californians and observers all across the country. Siding with Smith and Ghimenti were those who oppose abstinence-only programs and prefer comprehensive sex education, which includes teaching about birth control methods and in some places dispensing contraceptives. In this comprehensive approach, teachers strongly recommend that students practice abstinence until they are adults. But information about contraceptives is given, too, to help protect those teens who do not follow that advice.

A nurse counsels a young man in the proper use of condoms. Comprehensive sex education programs in the schools include frank discussions about birth control.

Smith, Ghimenti, and other like-minded people said that part of the problem was that Clovis's existing sex ed classes utilized an outdated and inaccurate textbook. It was titled *Lifetime Health*. According to the wording of the suit, the book "promotes the abstinence-only policy many states—but not California—pursued a decade ago." Moreover, the complaint stated, the textbook "teaches that people (including consenting adults) should refrain from sexual intimacy until they are married" and "omits any information about condoms and contraception."[45]

Not only did these teachings violate the 2003 state law, the opponents pointed out, the text had many inaccuracies and misleading statements. "Our kids need complete, accurate information to help them protect themselves against STDs and unintended pregnancy," Smith told the press. "That's information they'll need at whatever point in their life they become sexually active."[46]

The core of that information, she and other opponents said, consists of the fact that teens who use condoms and other contraceptives are less likely to get pregnant than those who do not use them. In comparison, they argued, simply urging adolescents not to have sex until they are married is unrealistic. Some of those young people will end up having sex anyway. Furthermore, Smith and the others contended, because they were not taught about birth control, they will not acquire and use contraceptives, and the result will be unwanted pregnancies.

Steering Clear of Temptation

On the other side of the suit, as well as the issue of abstinence-only education in general, were Clovis school district officials. Backing them were a number of local and state residents who felt that the district's stand for abstinence-only and against comprehensive sex ed was the right thing to do. In addressing the public, school district spokesperson Kelly Avants first emphasized that the materials and approach the Clovis district employed in its sex ed classes complied fully with state standards. She denied that the Clovis system had broken any state rules, saying, "We will continue our review of the suit in order to better understand the concerns raised by the plaintiffs, but Clovis Unified has fully complied with both the California Education Code and the State's content standards."[47]

In another statement, Avants claimed that the district was not out of touch with the most effective approaches to teaching sex ed. The people who put the program together had consulted experts, including scientists and physicians. Avants stated, "We have a very lengthy and transparent curriculum adoption process." She explained that this process involved not only parents and community members, but also "health and science teachers, curriculum administrators, and health practitioners."[48] Local supporters of the abstinence-only approach agreed with Avants's defense of the way the existing program put most of its stress on urging students to refrain from sexual relations.

TLW Promotes Moral Purity

In the past two decades, the youth-based international organization True Love Waits (TLW) has been in the forefront of the debate about the effectiveness of abstinence-only education. The group claims that it promotes moral purity by citing and trying to live by biblical principles and also by employing positive peer pressure. TLW's website provides some background information about its beginnings and successes to date:

> The first True Love Waits national celebration took place in July 1994, when more than 210,000 covenant cards were displayed on the National Mall in Washington, D.C. Today, an estimated 3 million youth have signed commitment cards pledging sexual purity until their wedding day, and that number continues to grow worldwide. Hundreds of thousands of commitment cards from youth throughout the world have been displayed at several events, including the 2004 Olympics in Athens. More than one hundred organizations have adopted the use of True Love Waits to promote sexual abstinence, in large part because they have seen how well the campaign works and the potential it has to reverse negative trends in communities. True Love Waits receives no taxpayer money, yet its message has made a profound impact in the United States as well as other parts of the world.

True Love Waits, "True Love Waits—an Overview." www.lifeway.com.

Among those supporters were several local religious leaders who were adamant in their belief that the current program was better for the students than any comprehensive sex ed programs. They argued that by teaching about condoms and other contraceptives and by making them available to students, such programs encourage young people to experiment with sex. By contrast, in stressing abstinence-only, the existing program in the Clovis schools tried to steer students away from the temptation to engage in sexual relations. Jim Franklin, pastor of Fresno's Cornerstone Church, told newspaper reporters, "We know that abstinence works. We know that is the number one hundred percent foolproof way of preventing teen pregnancy and preventing STDs."[49]

Sources of Funding

In a very real way, this clash of opinions in California's Clovis school district is a microcosm of a national debate that has received public attention for close to two decades. During those years, the same question has been raised again and again in school districts all across the country: Namely, should sex education cover various methods of birth control, or should it focus exclusively on abstinence?

Although no definitive answer to this question emerged during those years, social and political ideology consistently influenced preferences. With few exceptions, more conservative organizations and states tended to approve of and promote abstinence-only programs. Similarly, their progressive, or liberal, counterparts usually supported comprehensive sex ed programs.

For a long time, abstinence-only programs had a decided financial advantage over comprehensive sex ed programs. Until fairly recently the federal government funded only abstinence-only programs. Comprehensive sex ed programs had to make do with lesser amounts of funding from state and local governments.

Federal funding for abstinence-only programs began on a fairly modest scale in 1981–1982, at the outset of the administration of President Ronald Reagan. Financial support for abstinence-only programs remained moderate until 1996. In that year conservatives

"We know that abstinence works. We know that is the number one hundred percent foolproof way of preventing teen pregnancy and preventing STDs."[49]

— Jim Franklin, pastor of Cornerstone Church in Fresno, California.

in Congress pushed through a major increase in funding for these programs. These monies continued to grow, and the programs reached their peak of popularity during the years of President George W. Bush's administration—2001 to 2009. In the Bush era, government monies for abstinence-only programs ballooned from $73 million per year in 2001 to $204 million per year in 2008.

In 2010, however, during President Barack Obama's first term, federal funding for abstinence-only programs fell to $50 million a year. At the same time, some $190 million was allocated for comprehensive sex ed programs—the first time these programs had received funding on such a large scale.

Critiques of Abstinence-Only

The Obama administration made these changes after consulting with the CDC and other respected medical and public health organizations. These groups claimed that comprehensive sex ed programs had a credible chance of reducing teen pregnancy rates. In contrast, they said, their own recent studies had suggested that abstinence-only programs did not reduce those rates.

One of these studies was done by Janet E. Rosenbaum of the Johns Hopkins Bloomberg School of Public Health. She compared the sexual behavior over the course of a few years of adolescents who swore an oath of abstinence (such as the True Love Waits organization's pledge to refrain from sex until marriage) with that of teens who did not take the pledge. She found no difference in the sexual behavior of the teens in the two groups. About 82 percent of the young people who took the pledge broke it while still in their teens, and over time they, like those in the other group, had an average of three sexual partners. These findings, Rosenbaum said, suggested that abstinence-only programs were largely ineffective.

Supporters of abstinence-only sex education flatly rejected these findings. Some of them called Rosenbaum's methods faulty. Valerie Huber of the National Abstinence Education Association, for instance, stated that Rosenbaum "inaccurately equates the holistic breadth of an abstinence education program to the one-time event of a virginity pledge. A pledge and an abstinence program are not synonymous."[50]

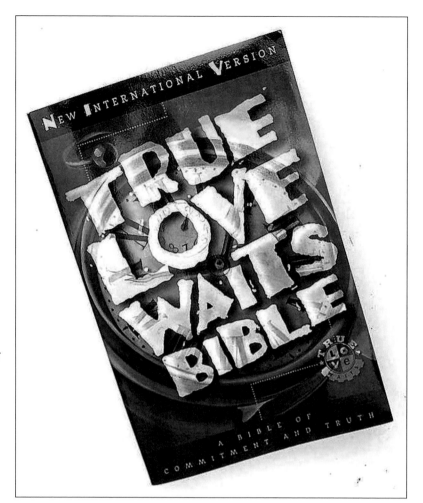

The True Love Waits campaign, created by a Christian organization, has encouraged thousands of US teenagers to make a commitment to sexual abstinence until marriage. Such pledges are sometimes a feature of abstinence-only education programs.

Number of Districts and Schools

The exact number of schools in the country that currently feature either abstinence-only programs or comprehensive sex ed programs is unclear. In 2002, when abstinence-only sex education was at its height of popularity, the Kaiser Family Foundation estimated that roughly two-thirds of the thirteen thousand–plus existing US school systems mandated the teaching of sex education. (The other third either left sex ed up to individual schools and teachers or had no sex ed at all.) Of the two-thirds of districts that required sex ed, the foundation found, about half used an abstinence-only approach. The other half featured comprehensive sex ed programs.

Evidence suggests that these rough numbers remain approximately the same today. The two kinds of programs are not evenly distributed across the nation, however. As might be expected, abstinence-only programs are found predominantly in conservative regions and states, and comprehensive sex ed programs exist mainly in more progressive ones. This explains why fully half of the school districts that have abstinence-only programs are in a handful of largely conservative southern states. By contrast, just 20 percent of abstinence-only programs can be found in the generally more liberal northeastern states.

A Point of Agreement

During the past few decades, as school systems did their best to find federal, state, or other funding for sex education programs, abstinence-only and comprehensive sex ed seemed to be the only two options. A closer examination of the issue, however, reveals that both approaches have one thing in common: Both emphasize the value of abstinence. The CDC estimates that about 87 percent of US public and private secondary schools currently teach that abstinence is the most effective method known to avoid pregnancy. (Most of the remaining schools do not require the teaching of a health education course that includes sex ed.)

Backers of both kinds of programs agree that most teenagers are not emotionally mature enough to be sexually active and that the incidence of teen pregnancy can be reduced by avoiding risky behavior. More specifically, as in other risk-avoidance behaviors, the underlying principle is that one cannot eliminate an unwanted behavior by acting on it sometimes. To be truly effective, one should avoid that behavior all the time. When trying to quit smoking, for instance, most experts agree that the most effective course is to quit altogether, not to smoke occasionally.

Persuasive support for this view comes from a 2006 study that still carries significant weight in the public health community. Kate Hendricks, vice president for science at the Medical Institute for Sexual Health, and four like-minded colleagues summarized the primary focus of their study, writing, "Abstinence education programs are based on the basic public health principle of primary prevention. They mirror other widely accepted youth-oriented programs that advocate risk avoidance strategies for drugs, alcohol, and tobacco. Few, if any, public health professionals would argue against abstinence as the healthiest behavior for school-aged children."[51]

Thus, both abstinence-only and comprehensive sex ed programs have at least one point of agreement. They each accept and promote the value of young people's abstaining from sex. The main difference between the two approaches is that comprehensive sex ed programs also include information about, and in some cases distribution of, contraceptives. In such programs abstinence is taught as one of several effective birth control methods. Noted *New York Times* columnist Gail Collins describes the reasoning behind this approach, saying, "The only foolproof way to avoid pregnancy is, of course, not to have sex. But once that horse is out of the barn, there doesn't seem to be any effective way to get kids to refrain from having it again. That's the point at which it becomes important that they understand the dangers of unprotected sex, and that sex with a condom is far, far safer than sex with nothing at all."[52]

Strengthening Society as a Whole

Although people on both sides of the issue concur that abstinent behavior for teens is effective and to be desired, they agree on little else. First and foremost, those who back the abstinence-only approach feel that teaching about contraception has no place at all in sex ed programs. At the heart of this contention is the belief that introducing young people to birth control methods and devices will encourage them to have sex. A spokesperson for the National Abstinence Education Foundation, based in Washington, DC, states the position this way:

Comprehensive sex ed programs use explicit demonstrations to teach contraception usage skills. The commentary accompanying many of these demonstrations refers to sexual activity as "fun" in a way that trivializes the inherent risks along with a tone of tacit endorsement that communicates sexual activity among teens as "normal" and expected. The explicit nature of these demonstrations crosses the line between factual education and actual provocative promotion, demonstrating a violation of the need to educate, not advocate.[53]

Instead, the foundation and other supporters of abstinence-only say, schools should present students with facts about how abstinence prevents both pregnancy and the spread of STDs, along

Learning to Think Critically

Konstance McCaffree of Widener University's Human Sexuality Program advocates teaching children and young adults about both abstinence and birth control. As she explains here, she believes this approach will help young people learn to think more critically.

> The belief that we should only send one message to our children implies that it would then be the only message that they would receive. If we are talking about sexual activity and arguing for abstinence-only, then in many ways we are ignoring the other messages and desires that teens have and preventing them from processing their feelings about the other messages. The advantage of talking with children about several options is that it helps them to think critically about the situation so that when they are in situations where there is temptation to act in ways that may be risky, they have the ability to consider alternatives and to examine what the outcomes can be.

Konstance McCaffree, "Can We Talk About Abstinence and Contraception or Is It a Mixed Message?," Advocates for Youth, 2008. www.advocatesforyouth.org.

with a set of values. The latter should include not only the point that refraining from sexual activity is a good thing, but also certain constructive social beliefs and customs. When it greatly increased funding for abstinence-only programs in 1996, Congress also mandated an eight-point definition of those programs that included such values. Among them was that two young people who enter into a relationship should form a faithful monogamous bond. Further, that bond should be the accepted standard of human sexual and marriage relationships. Moreover, the 1996 abstinence-only definition states, having sex outside of marriage will almost always be harmful to those who practice it.

In this way, supporters maintain, abstinence-only programs do more than prevent pregnancy and help young people perform better in their daily lives. They also promote behavior that will hopefully strengthen the institution of marriage and with it society as a whole. "Children in families whose parents are married have better emotional and physical health," the National Abstinence Education Foundation says as part of its promotion of abstinence-only education. Those teens also "have more opportunities to achieve academically, and enjoy improved life outcomes. Thus, due to their ability to shape happiness and well-being, marriage and family are two of the most important institutions in society, and the existence of healthy relationships within these institutions is a key factor that determines its vitality."[54]

Teaching Both?

Many of the critics of abstinence-only education say that these social goals are inappropriate for any sex ed programs. Goals of that sort, they state, along with the notion that people should remain virgins until they are married, are part of a hidden religious agenda. Debra Hauser, executive vice president of Advocates for Youth, a group that encourages young people to make informed, effective decisions, argues that this agenda endorses conservative Christian values. There is nothing wrong with waiting till marriage to have sex, she emphasizes. Nor is it misguided to want to strengthen the marriage institution. However, she cautions, not everyone can or wants to aspire to these aims. What is more, morality-based goals deriving from a specific faith or religious denomination should not be forced on all students in a public school setting.

Hauser has other objections to the fact that abstinence-only instruction is religion or morality based. For instance, she points out, such instruction implies that those young people who are unable to live up to its ideals—the ones who give in and have sex—have somehow failed. So they should feel shame, a concept that is intrinsic to morality-based systems. Responding to a 2012 congressional attempt to allocate $5 million to revive an abstinence-only education program that had earlier been canceled, she stated, "I am shocked that Congress would fund programs that ignore science and teach young people fear, shame, and denial. Parents, medical experts, and young people agree that schools have a responsibility to provide sex education that includes information about both abstinence and contraception."[55]

Another strong advocate of sex ed programs that teach both abstinence and contraception is Konstance McCaffree, sexuality education coordinator at Widener University in Pennsylvania. When asked for her opinion on the subject, she often recalls the words of a former student, who told her, "Hearing about both abstinence and contraception helped me make a more responsible sexual decision. Had I not had a class where both were presented, a thorough discussion between my partner and I would probably never have taken place. I knew after hearing all the considerations that we were not ready for the responsibility."[56]

> "Parents, medical experts, and young people agree that schools have a responsibility to provide sex education that includes information about both abstinence and contraception."[55]
>
> — Debra Hauser, executive vice president of Advocates for Youth.

Not Easily Dismissed

Hauser and McCaffree are mistaken to think that teaching *both* abstinence and contraception is the best approach, states John B. Jemmott of the University of Pennsylvania. In a 2010 study, he held three sex education classes for middle school students. One taught abstinence-only, the second solely discussed birth control, and the third combined both approaches. The results were that only about a third of those in the abstinence-only class had sex in the two years that followed. In contrast, half of the students in the birth control class and 42 percent of those in the combination class had sex in the same period. Jemmott and other abstinence-only advocates hail the study as proof that their approach to sex ed works better than the comprehensive sex ed approach.

The fact that seemingly convincing arguments and studies have been and continue to be presented by both sides of the debate brings two things into sharp focus. First, the issue of abstinence-only versus comprehensive sex education is highly complex, and one side cannot and should not presume to easily dismiss the other. Second, advocates on both sides of the issue are well-meaning and passionate. They are equally concerned for the future well-being of the nation and its youth, and they and their respective views should be accorded serious attention in the years ahead.

Facts

- Twenty-nine states, along with Puerto Rico, currently fund abstinence-only education programs in schools, according to the Congressional Research Service.

- The Guttmacher Institute states that in 2002 about 90 percent of publicly funded family planning clinics counseled clients younger than eighteen about abstinence.

- In recent years, according to the CDC, about 65 percent of teen girls and 53 percent of teen boys have taken sex education classes mentioning both abstinence and birth control.

- About 44 percent of girls and 27 percent of boys say they have spoken with their parents about both abstinence and birth control, the CDC reports.

- According to the Kaiser Family Foundation, 82 percent of parents who have children aged eighteen and younger support schools that teach both comprehensive sex ed and abstinence.

How Does Access to Contraception Affect Teen Pregnancy Rates?

Among the core issues in the larger debate over giving teens access to contraceptives, none is more controversial and has more potential to harm both adolescents and society as a whole than unintended teen pregnancy. According to the CDC and other reputable organizations, about 750,000 teenage women become pregnant each year. Of those pregnancies, roughly 82 percent, or 615,000, are unplanned.

The CDC also notes that such unintentional pregnancies almost always have serious physical, emotional, and economic costs. About 50 percent of teenage mothers fail to graduate from high school before age twenty-two, for example. Also, far fewer teen mothers are able to hold down jobs than are teen girls who have no children. Moreover, babies born to adolescent mothers are more likely to die in infancy, and female children born to teen mothers are about 33 percent more likely to later become teen mothers themselves. What is more, the CDC continues, teen pregnancies and births cost American taxpayers enormous amounts of money.

These expenses include $3 billion a year in health care, $6 billion in lost taxes, and nearly $3 billion in other public costs.

Considering these facts, people on both sides of the debate agree that too many teenage girls have unplanned pregnancies each year. Various remedies have been proposed to deal with the problem. But by far the most common one put forward in recent years has been to give young people access to birth control. That effort has itself ignited a controversy over how it actually affects teen pregnancy rates. Advocates claim that providing young people with contraceptives results in fewer pregnancies, whereas opponents say it causes more problems than it solves.

A Bold Move in Denver

Arguments of this sort accompanied a number of earnest attempts to address the teen pregnancy dilemma by making birth control available to American young people. One of the more publicized efforts in this regard occurred in Denver, Colorado, in 2010. In that year the Bruce Randolph School, a public educational facility for sixth through twelfth graders, became the city's first school to give its students access to contraceptives. In a bold move the school's health clinic, situated within the main building, made condoms, birth control pills, and emergency contraception accessible to those students whose parents had previously signed them up for the new program.

The decision to allow the clinic to dispense contraceptives was not a sudden, spontaneous move but rather was three years in the making. Back in 2007 concerned school officials, parents, and others in the community formed a committee and began meeting to discuss ways to reduce the local teen pregnancy rate. At the time, that rate in Denver was nearly twice as high as it was for the entire state. Colorado's teen pregnancy rate was then about twenty-two per one thousand girls aged fifteen to seventeen. Compared with that, Denver's rate of about forty-one per one thousand was seen as troubling and unacceptable.

Even worse, the committee found, from 2007 to 2010, when the new birth control distribution program was instituted, the pregnancy rate for Hispanic teens in Denver was almost 3.5 times

higher than that for all girls in the entire state—approximately seventy-seven new babies per one thousand girls. An outspoken Denver mother, Jennifer Gonzalez, was worried that these and other local teen mothers were less likely to finish high school, attend college, or end up with well-paying jobs. She remarked:

A young mother studies for school while holding her two-year-old daughter. Advocates of greater teen access to birth control believe such access will help reduce unplanned pregnancies among teenagers.

> We have a whole generation of kids who are being raised by teen parents who don't want their children to go through what we went through. I don't want to see my kids go through that. It's hard. We struggle every day. We go paycheck to paycheck. We don't own a home, can't afford vacation and all the things my teenage kids want. I don't want them to have anything to hold them back from their dreams.[57]

For these reasons, Gonzalez explained, she was willing to give the proposed contraceptive program a try. She was not alone. The

Bruce Randolph School's principal, Cesar Cedillo, pointed out that thirteen female students had unplanned babies between 2008 and 2010. In 2009, moreover, five of the school's seniors were teen mothers. "That's an incredible number," Cedillo said, referring to the fact that of the school's roughly eight hundred students, only a little more than one hundred are seniors in a given year. "It is absolutely heartbreaking,"[58] he added.

Tina Maestas agreed. A mother with two daughters in the school and a big local booster of the new school birth control program, she stated forcefully, "Any amount of appropriate education and access is not only going to be beneficial for the youth but to their family and our community in general. It's not a blessing for them or giving them the permission to go have sex. Kids are going to have sex anyway."[59]

More, Not Fewer, Pregnancies?

As the dispute over the new program at Bruce Randolph erupted, a number of Denver residents spoke up to say that they could not disagree more with Maestas. "Any amount" of access to birth control would *not* be beneficial to students, they insisted. Nor was it true, in their view, that teens are bound to have sex no matter what messages they get from parents, teachers, and others.

Among the staunchest of these opponents was Lolita Hanks, a nurse practitioner and member of Colorado Right to Life, a prominent local antiabortion group. She warned that distributing condoms and other contraceptives to young people would be extremely counterproductive. "It's just going to cause more sexual activity,"[60] she asserted. Hanks admitted that she herself had gotten pregnant when she was a teenager. Allowing young teens to get their hands on contraceptives, she believes, would send a message to them that it is all right to experiment with sex.

That, in turn, would almost certainly lead to *more* teen pregnancies, not fewer, Hanks continued. By giving sixth graders access to birth control, she said, "you

"Any amount of appropriate education and access [to contraceptives] is not only going to be beneficial for the youth but to their family and our community in general."[59]

— Tina Maestas, a mother with two daughters in Denver's Bruce Randolf School.

are telling me that they are mature enough to be compliant with birth control, and that they are mature enough to have children, which is a result of having sex."[61] Surely, Hanks said, no responsible adult could make that argument.

Plummeting Teen Birthrates

A similar debate about how providing teens access to contraceptives can affect their pregnancy rates occurred between 2010 and 2012 in Alexandria, Virginia. When the new on-campus Teen Wellness Center opened at T.C. Williams High School in 2010, it began distributing condoms and other contraceptives to students who requested them. The program caused a controversy in the community, the state, and beyond.

One of the main reasons for instituting the new birth control program was a desire among school system officials and concerned members of the community to reduce the rate of student pregnancies. One of those who thought the program would turn out to be beneficial was David Wynne, the high school's social worker. Two years later he said he felt he had been vindicated. In April 2012 he pointed out that the number of annual teen pregnancies in the community had decreased between 2010 and 2012. It went from fifty down to thirty-five pregnancies in the first year, he said, and from thirty-five to twenty pregnancies in the second year. In Wynne's view, this reduction in pregnancies occurred because having the clinic inside the school made student access to it easier. Even more important, he suggested, was that more of the students gained access to contraceptives and used them.

Wynne and other advocates of the new contraceptive distribution policy believe this decrease in unplanned pregnancies among Alexandria's teens mirrors what has been happening on the national level in recent years. They point to statistics compiled by the CDC, Washington University (in St. Louis, Missouri), and other widely trusted sources. For example, in 2012 the CDC's National Center for Health Statistics reported the results of a survey that examined teen birthrates in large numbers of US school districts. The survey's starting point was the early 1990s, before the policy of giving adolescents contraceptives began to be widely

The Right Way

The birth control distribution program at Denver's Bruce Randolph School was originally devised by a small group of Colorado doctors. One of them was David Kaplan, chief of adolescent medicine at Children's Hospital in Aurora, Colorado, and a teacher of pediatrics at the University of Colorado School of Medicine. Back in 1989 these doctors first discussed the issue of the high numbers of teen pregnancies in the state, and especially in Denver, and how they might be reduced. They agreed that in-school clinics that dispensed contraceptives seemed to be a promising approach. But they realized that at the time, giving teens access to birth control would have been far too controversial. "It was our sense that offering reproductive health services would really be inflammatory," Kaplan says. As a result, "We really tried to steer away from that."

Between 2007 and 2010, however, large numbers of parents gave their support to such a program. This greatly encouraged Kaplan and the other physicians because they knew that getting parents to agree with a birth control policy for teens was a major key to making that program a success. "I think it is happening the right way," he says.

Quoted in Jeremy P. Meyer, "School Is Denver's First to Offer Contraceptives in Fight Against Teen Births," *Denver Post.com*, August 22, 2010. www.denverpost.com.

implemented. The survey found that in 1991 teen birthrates were disturbingly high—more than seventy births for each one thousand teen girls.

The survey also looked at the number of teens having babies in 2010 (the latest year for which national statistics are available). It found that birthrates among girls aged fifteen to nineteen had plummeted to thirty-four for each one thousand. That translated into a whopping 44 percent drop in teen pregnancies and births in the United States between 1991 and 2010. It was the lowest these rates had been since 1946, a year after the close of World War II. In addition, the survey showed that the decreases in the numbers of teen pregnancies and births occurred in all the racial and ethnic groups, as well as in almost all the states. Large numbers of scientists and other researchers attributed these reduced birthrates to the steady rise of comprehensive sex ed, including providing some teens access to birth control.

Fewer Young Women Having Sex?

Not everyone who looked at these figures drew the same conclusions, however. A number of observers both inside and outside of Alexandria disagreed that the reduction in teen pregnancies at T.C. Williams, as well as nationally, was chiefly the result of giving teens access to birth control. Those who felt this policy was a mistake argued that its so-called benefits remain unproven. Although the observed reduction in the number of pregnancies nationwide was certainly a good thing, they said, it may have been caused by a combination of other factors.

One such factor cited by opponents of the contraceptive policy was a misunderstanding of who was with child and when. In this view, many pregnant teens do not "show," or appear to be carrying a baby, until the last few months before delivery. Also, a number of those deliveries occur in late summer, before the school year starts. So at least some girls who got pregnant did not get counted in the fall, when the survey collected its data, and the decline in the number of pregnancies was not as high as that study claimed.

Another possible reason for the nationwide decrease in pregnancy rates, the policy's opponents say, is that fewer students may have engaged in sex during the decades in question. One strong piece of evidence that may support this view comes from the results of a recent CDC study of data collected by the National Survey of Family Growth. Among these results, which were announced in 2011, was the revelation that indeed, fewer teenage girls had sexual relations during the past few years than in earlier decades. In the period from 2006 to 2010, the data showed, 57 percent of girls aged fifteen to nineteen said they had never had vaginal intercourse. That figure was a full eight points higher than

it had been back in 1995. In that year the National Survey recorded that only 49 percent of girls in the same age group reported never having had vaginal sex.

Fewer teenage girls were having sex in the years leading up to 2010, opponents of the birth control distribution policy say. So the number of teen pregnancies and live births quite naturally went down. There is therefore no need to attribute the drop to the fact that young people had more access to contraceptives. "These trends are so encouraging," the National Abstinence Education Association's Valerie Huber exclaimed in October 2011. "They are moving in the right direction," she pointed out, toward more abstinent behavior by teens. Without a doubt, the new data "demonstrates that the sexual risk-avoidance approach is resonating with teens, and they are responding by increasingly choosing to wait for sex." Huber then pointedly asked, "Why is there no meaningful emphasis on sexual risk-avoidance in current public policy? Shouldn't we be reinforcing this healthy behavior in any way we can? Instead, at every turn, there is a message that is normalizing teen sex and teen sexual experimentation."[62]

Federal Government's Controversial Move

Not long after the release of the CDC study showing an increase in abstinence among teenage girls, Huber and other opponents of giving contraceptives to adolescents had even more reason to be encouraged. In December 2011 the secretary of the US Department of Health and Human Services, Kathleen Sebelius, halted sales of the Plan B birth control pill, or emergency contraception, over the counter without a doctor's prescription. The move was aimed at young girls. Had she not acted when she did, girls as young as eleven or twelve would have been allowed to walk into any pharmacy and buy Plan B, the contraceptive substance that in most cases prevents pregnancy if taken soon after a girl has unprotected sex.

Justifying her move, Sebelius stated that the drug's manufacturer, Teva Pharmaceuticals, had not studied its possible side effects on girls as young as eleven. So there was no guarantee that it was safe for children that young to use. "After careful consideration of the FDA summary review," she said, "I have concluded that the data submitted by Teva do not conclusively establish that Plan B One-Step should be made available over the counter for all girls of reproductive age."[63]

Hoping to Change Teen Behavior

Bill Albert, chief program officer at the National Campaign to Prevent Teen and Unplanned Pregnancy, headed that organization's 2012 survey on the teen pregnancy issue. He drew a number of conclusions from the answers that teens and parents gave to his questions, including the following:

> Even though U.S. teen pregnancy and birth rates are at historic lows, the clear majority of adults nationwide believe more needs to be done in their community to help prevent teen pregnancy. Smart thinking. Despite the impressive progress all 50 states have made in preventing too-early pregnancy and parenthood, it remains the case that nearly three in 10 girls get pregnant by age 20. It is also worth noting that adults see a clear role for the federal government in preventing teen pregnancy. As a general matter, taxpayers want federally funded efforts to prevent teen pregnancy to encourage young people to delay sex and provide them with information about birth control. They also want to be sure that their money is well spent; investing only in those efforts that have been shown through careful evaluation to actually change teen behavior.

Bill Albert, "With One Voice 2012: America's Adults and Teens Sound Off About Teen Pregnancy," National Campaign to Prevent Teen and Unplanned Pregnancy, August 2012. www.the nationalcampaign.org.

There was general support for Sebelius's move among conservative individuals and groups. One of their typical responses was that young girls had no business taking such powerful drugs, even if the goal was to reduce the annual number of teen pregnancies. Jeanne Monahan of the Family Research Council, a conservative advocacy group, praised the decision, saying, "Secretary Kathleen Sebelius was right to reject the FDA recommendation to make this potent drug available over the counter to young girls."[64]

On the flip side, reactions by progressive individuals and groups to Sebelius's decision were mostly critical. Some agreed

A health professional counsels a teenager. According to a 2012 survey by the National Campaign to Prevent Teen and Unplanned Pregnancy, many teens would rather learn about both abstinence and contraceptives as opposed to only learning about one or the other.

with her that it was too risky to allow younger girls to take Plan B at this time. It would be better to wait, they said, until further research had confirmed it was safe for women of all ages.

Many others were more cynical, however. They suggested that Sebelius kept Plan B behind the counter because high-placed officials in the Obama reelection campaign had urged her to do it. A *Los Angeles Times* editorial cited suspicions within some reproductive rights groups "that the decision was politically motivated, perhaps by fear within the Obama administration of being attacked during the presidential campaign for encouraging young girls to have unprotected sex without their parents' knowledge."[65] The leader of one of the groups mentioned in the editorial, Kirsten Moore, president of the Reproductive Health Technologies Project, objected strenuously to Sebelius's move. "We are outraged," she stated, "that this administration has let politics trump science."[66]

In addition, the American Academy of Pediatrics weighed in on the side of the critics. It issued a new position paper on November 26, 2012. Published online by the *Journal of Pediatrics,* the paper said that it would be prudent for doctors to give underage teens prescriptions for Plan B-type contraceptives before they start having sex. In their view, this would be the most effective way to prevent unplanned teen pregnancies.

Is Peaceful Coexistence Possible?

A few observers pointed out that no matter what motivated Sebelius's decision, it was almost certain that Plan B would eventually be available over the counter without a prescription. If it was indeed a matter of safety, the manufacturer would find a way to tweak the drug in the appropriate manner. If, by contrast, the decision to keep Plan B behind the counter was political in nature, officials in the Obama administration would wait until they felt the time was right and get the Department of Health and Human Services to reverse the directive. Either way, in this view, one of the most potent of the existing contraceptives will sooner or later become available to teens of all ages.

If that scenario does come to pass, it will surely make the ongoing debate over teen pregnancy and how access to birth control affects it even more contentious and bitter than it already is. Each side will, no doubt, continue to assert that the other is wrong. It will also insist that its own position will reduce teen pregnancies and is therefore healthier in the long run for America's youth.

Yet as sexual health researcher Martha Kempner suggests, the two sides are not necessarily incompatible. It is generally a fairly small number of politicians and members of organizations with political, religious, and media agendas, she says, who choose a side and dig in their heels, so to speak. When many average people "are asked about this topic," Kempner points out, "it turns out that they take the pretty rational view that abstinence and contraception can and should peacefully coexist."[67]

Kempner calls attention to a 2012 survey by the widely respected National Campaign to Prevent Teen and Unplanned Pregnancy. It asked both adults and teens some general questions about sex, contraception, and teen pregnancy, and some of the answers, she says, are very revealing. In particular, she cited the question "Do you wish you/teens were getting more information about abstinence, more information about birth control or protection, or more information about both?"[68] An overwhelming 74 percent of adults and 49 percent of teens said both. (Only 13 percent of adults and 7 percent of teens said abstinence, and just 9 percent of adults and 13 percent of teens said birth control or protection.)

The survey's author, Bill Albert, agrees that most Americans sense that the answer to the teen pregnancy problem involves some kind of combination of abstinence and birth control use. "The extraordinary progress that the nation has made in reducing teen pregnancy and childbearing in the past two decades," he states, "has been driven by a combination of less sex and more contraception." So educating teens about both is a "common sense approach."[69]

"The extraordinary progress that the nation has made in reducing teen pregnancy and childbearing in the past two decades has been driven by a combination of less sex and more contraception."[69]

— Bill Albert of the National Campaign to Prevent Teen and Unplanned Pregnancy.

Facts

- The CDC states that the US teen pregnancy rate has fallen 44 percent since 1991.

- According to Planned Parenthood, teenage mothers are less likely to graduate from high school and more likely than women who wait till adulthood to have children to live in poverty and to receive welfare payments.

- The Guttmacher Institute says that teens account for about 20 percent of all unintended pregnancies in the United States each year.

- The US teen pregnancy rate for women aged fifteen to nineteen is one of the highest in the developed world, reports the Congressional Research Service.

- According to the CDC, about 43 percent of US teenage girls have had sexual relations, thereby risking pregnancy.

Source Notes

Introduction: Differing Approaches to a Real Crisis

1. Quoted in Dr. Phil, "Teens and Birth Control, Part Two," *Turning Point* (blog), September 26, 2009. http://blog.drphil.com.
2. Quoted in Dr. Phil, "Teens and Birth Control, Part Two."
3. Project Cap, "Teen Pregnancy—the Importance of Prevention," April 8, 2011. http://projectcap.org.
4. Quoted in Brandi Laren, "Statistics on Teen Pregnancy," eHow. www.ehow.com.
5. Edward Sztukowski and Lynn Schwebach, "Teenage Pregnancy Prevention," All Psychology Careers.com. www.allpsychologycareers.com.
6. Sztukowski and Lynn Schwebach, "Teenage Pregnancy Prevention."

Chapter One: How Did the Availability of Birth Control to Teens Become Controversial?

7. Kathleen London, "The History of Birth Control," Yale–New Haven Teachers Institute, 2012. www.yale.edu.
8. London, "The History of Birth Control."
9. Johannah Cornblatt, "The Evolution of Birth Control," Daily Beast, October 28, 2009. www.thedailybeast.com.
10. Gary F. Kelly, *America's Sexual Transformation: How the Sexual Revolution's Legacy Is Shaping Our Society, Our Youth, and Our Future.* Santa Barbara, CA: ABC-CLIO, 2012, p. 8.
11. Quoted in *U.S. News & World Report*, "The Pill: How It Is Affecting U.S. Morals, Family Life," July 11, 1966, p. 62.
12. Quoted in *U.S. News & World Report*, "The Pill."
13. John C. McWilliams. *The 1960s Cultural Revolution.* Westport, CT: Greenwood, 2000, pp. 1–2.
14. McWilliams, *The 1960s Cultural Revolution*, p. 16.
15. Nancy L. Cohen, "How the Sexual Revolution Changed America Forever," AlterNet, February 5, 2012. www.alternet.org.
16. R. Albert Mohler Jr., "Why the Sexual Revolution Needed a Sexual Revolutionary," *Atlantic*, August 23, 2012. www.theatlantic.com.
17. Cohen, "How the Sexual Revolution Changed America Forever."

Chapter Two: Should Schools Make Birth Control Available to Teens?

18. Patrick Welsh, "Schools Dispensing Birth Control," *USA Today*, April 4, 2012. http://usatoday30.usatoday.com.

19. Quoted in Michael Lee Pope, "Birth-Control Center Finds Home in T.C.," *Alexandria (VA) Gazette Packet*, March 11, 2010. http://connection.membershipsoftware.org.

20. University of Wisconsin Population Health Institute, "Condom Availability Programs," April 11, 2011. http://whatworksforhealth.wisc.edu.

21. Quoted in Jack Nicas, "Condoms Old News in Many Schools," Boston.com, June 28, 2010. www.boston.com.

22. Greg Pfundstein, "The Misguided Birth Control Debate Continues," *National Review*, August 2, 2011. http://www.nationalreview.com.

23. Sally Guttmacher et al., "Condom Availability in New York City Public High Schools: Relationships to Condom Use and Sexual Behavior," *American Journal of Public Health,* September 1997, p. 1432.

24. Rebecca Mikulin, "Should Schools Give Teens Birth Control?," Helium, September 22, 2008. www.helium.com.

25. Rosemary Redfern, "Should Schools Give Teens Birth Control?," Helium, January 10, 2009. www.helium.com.

26. Quoted in Lindsey Tanner and Karen Matthews, "New York Schools Dispensing Birth Control," *Salt Lake City (UT) Deseret News*, September 25, 2012. www.deseretnews.com.

27. New York City Parents' Choice Coalition, "Open Letter to Mayor Bloomberg and Chancellor Walcott." www.nycparentschoice.org.

28. Quoted in CBS New York, "Mayor Michael Bloomberg Defends Giving NYC Students Plan B 'Morning-After Pill.'" September 24, 2012. http://newyork.cbslocal.com.

29. Quoted in *USA Today*, "Morning-After Pills Available at 13 NYC Public Schools," September 26, 2012. http://usatoday30.usatoday.com.

30. Rich Lowry, "New York City Schools' Birth Control Obsession," Newsmax, September 25, 2012. www.newsmax.com.

Chapter Three: Should Parental Consent Be Required for Teens Who Want Birth Control?

31. New York City Department of Health and Mental Hygiene, "CATCH Opt-Out Letter," New York City Parents' Choice Coalition, August 2011. www.nycparentschoice.org.

32. New York City Parents' Choice Coalition, "Press Release: NYC CATCH Program Poll." http://nycparentschoice.org.

33. Lowry, "New York City Schools' Birth Control Obsession."

34. Joyce Slaton, "New York Schools Give Birth Control Without Parents' Consent," *BabyCenter Blog*, September 24, 2012. http://blogs.babycenter.com.

35. Quoted in *USA Today*, "Morning-After Pills Available at 13 NYC Public Schools."

36. Center for Reproductive Rights, "Parental Consent and Notice for Contraceptives Threatens Teen Health and Constitutional Rights," November 1, 2006. http://reproductiverights.org.

37. Rachel K. Jones and Heather Boonstra, "Confidential Reproductive Health Services for Minors: The Potential Impact of Mandated Parental Involvement for Contraception," *Perspectives on Sexual and Reproductive Health*, 2004, pp. 182–183.

38. Supreme Court of Texas, "*Patterson v. Planned Parenthood of Houston and Southeast Texas, Inc.*," FindLaw, June 23, 1998. http://caselaw.findlaw.com.

39. Center for Reproductive Rights, "Parental Consent and Notice for Contraceptives Threatens Teen Health and Constitutional Rights."

40. Quoted in Austin Kline, "Parental Notification for Contraceptives?," About.com, June 25, 2005. http://atheism.about.com.

41. National Health Law Program, "The Parents' Right to Know Act Threatens Adolescent Health," Summer 2005. www.healthlaw.org.

42. Quoted in Sharon Jayson, "Expert: Risky Teen Behavior Is All in the Brain," *USA Today*, April 5, 2007. http://usatoday30.usatoday.com.

43. Annette Lamb, "Social Technology & Digital Citizenships: Rights, Responsibilities, and Ethical Behavior," Eduscapes, November 2010. www.eduscapes.com.

Chapter Four: Should Abstinence Be the Sole Birth Control Method Taught to Teens?

44. Quoted in Institute for Youth and Development, "California State Law: California Comprehensive Sexual Health and HIV/AIDS Prevention Education Act," 2004. www.youthdevelopment.org.

45. Superior Court of the State of California, County of Fresno, "*American Academy of Pediatrics, California District IX, Gay-Straight Alliance Network, Aubree Smith, and Mica Ghimenti, vs. Clovis Unified School District*," August 21, 2012. www.aclunc.org.

46. Quoted in ACLU of Northern California, "Parents and Doctors Sue Clovis School District over Sex Education," August 21, 2012. www.aclunc.org.

47. Quoted in Sevil Omer, "California School District Sued over Abstinence-Only Sex Ed," U.S. News, NBC News.com, August 23, 2012. http://usnews.nbcnews.com.

48. Quoted in Mariana Jacob, "Clovis Unified Sued over Sex Education Classes," ABC News, August 22, 2012. http://abclocal.go.com.

49. Quoted in Jacob, ABC News, "Clovis Unified Sued over Sex Education Classes."

50. Quoted in *Pennsylvania Conservative* (blog), "Predictable Lies About Abstinence Education from the *Washington Post*," December 31, 2008. http://pennsylvaniaconservative.blogspot.com.

51. Kate Hendricks et al., "The Attack on Abstinence Education: Fact or Fallacy?," Heartbeat International, May 5, 2005. www.heartbeatinternational.org.

52. Gail Collins, "Gail Collins on Texas's Abstinence Sex Education Problems," Daily Beast, June 4, 2012. www.thedailybeast.com.

53. National Abstinence Education Foundation, "Uncovering Comprehensive Sex Education," 2012. www.abstinenceworks.org.

54. National Abstinence Education Foundation, "Stats and Facts," 2012. www.abstinenceworks.org.

55. Quoted in SIECUS, "House Attempts to Revive Failed Community-Based Abstinence-Only-Until-Marriage Programs," December 15, 2011. www.siecus.org.

56. Quoted in Konstance McCaffree, "Can We Talk About Abstinence and Contraception or Is It a Mixed Message?," Advocates for Youth, 2008. www.advocatesforyouth.org.

Chapter Five: How Does Access to Contraception Affect Teen Pregnancy Rates?

57. Quoted in Jeremy P. Meyer, "School Is Denver's First to Offer Contraceptives in Fight Against Teen Births," *Denver Post*, August 22, 2010. www.denverpost.com.

58. Quoted in Meyer, "School Is Denver's First to Offer Contraceptives in Fight Against Teen Births."

59. Quoted in Meyer, "School Is Denver's First to Offer Contraceptives in Fight Against Teen Births."

60. Quoted in Meyer, "School Is Denver's First to Offer Contraceptives in Fight Against Teen Births."

61. Quoted in Meyer, "School Is Denver's First to Offer Contraceptives in Fight Against Teen Births."

62. Quoted in Cheryl Wetzstein, "Study Finds Teens Postponing Sex, Using Birth Control More," *Washington Times*, October 12, 2011. www.washingtontimes.com.

63. Quoted in Gardiner Harris, "Plan to Widen Availability of Morning-After Pill Is Rejected," *New York Times*, December 11, 2011. www.nytimes.com.

64. Quoted in Harris, "Plan to Widen Availability of Morning-After Pill Is Rejected."

65. *Los Angeles Times*, "Second-Guessing Plan B," editorial, December 8, 2011. http://articles.latimes.com.

66. Quoted in Harris, "Plan to Widen Availability of Morning-After Pill Is Rejected."

67. Martha Kempner, "New Survey Sheds Light on Americans' Attitudes About Teen Pregnancy and Sex," *RH Reality Check*, April 28, 2012. www.rhrealitycheck.org.

68. Quoted in Kempner, "New Survey Sheds Light on Americans' Attitudes About Teen Pregnancy and Sex."

69. Quoted in Kempner, "New Survey Sheds Light on Americans' Attitudes About Teen Pregnancy and Sex."

Related Organizations and Websites

Birth Control Watch

401 Ninth St. NW, Suite 450
Washington, DC 20004-2142
phone: (202) 326-8700
fax: (202) 682-2154
e-mail: birthcontrolwatch@ccmc.org
website: www.birthcontrolwatch.org/press_room.html

Birth Control Watch is a nonprofit organization that supports and promotes programs assisting women's quests for economic independence, including the ability to control their own reproduction by using birth control to avoid pregnancy.

Center for Reproductive Rights

1634 Eye St. NW, Suite 550
Washington, DC 20006
phone: (202) 628-0286
fax: (917) 637-3666
e-mail: info@reprorights.org
website: http://reproductiverights.org

The Center for Reproductive Rights works to bring about a world where every woman is free to decide whether and when to have children, has access to the best reproductive health care available, and can exercise her choices without coercion or discrimination.

Concerned Women for America (CWA)

1015 Fifteenth St. NW, Suite 1100
Washington, DC 20005
phone: (202) 488-7000
fax: (202) 488-0806
e-mail: mail@cwfa.org
website: www.cwfa.org/main.asp

The mission of the CWA is to protect and promote biblical values among all citizens through prayer and education, in order to reverse the decline in the nation's moral values—exemplified, among other things, by disturbingly high rates of teen pregnancy.

Family Research Council (FRC)

801 G St. NW
Washington, DC 20001
phone: (202) 393-2100
fax: (202) 393-2134
e-mail: http://usconservatives.about.com
website: http://usconservatives.about.com

The FRC advocates faith, family, and freedom in public policy and the culture from a Christian worldview. It promotes core values such as young women waiting until they are married to have sex and get pregnant.

Guttmacher Institute

125 Maiden Ln., 7th Floor
New York, NY 10038
phone: (212) 248-1111
toll-free: (800) 355-0244
fax: (212) 248-1951
e-mail: applytoguttmacher@guttmacher.org
website: www.guttmacher.org/index.html

The institute promotes sexual and reproductive health and rights using a program of public education, research, and policy analysis intended to offer new ideas and encourage public debate. Among the reproductive rights it supports is the right of teenagers to obtain and use birth control.

The Heritage Foundation
214 Massachusetts Ave. NE
Washington, DC 20002-4999
phone: (202) 546-4400
fax: (202) 546-8328
e-mail: info@heritage.org
website: www.heritage.org

The Heritage Foundation's mission is to formulate and promote conservative public policies based on the principles of free enterprise, individual freedom, and traditional American values, including the right of parents to oversee whether or not their children use contraceptives.

NARAL Pro-Choice America
1156 Fifteenth St. NW, Suite 700
Washington, DC 20005
phone: (202) 973-3000
fax: (202) 973-3096
e-mail: can@prochoiceamerica.org
website: www.prochoiceamerica.org

NARAL Pro-Choice America organizes men and women and lobbies Congress to protect women's right to choose whether or not to end a pregnancy and supports comprehensive sex education, including information about birth control, in schools.

National Campaign to Prevent Teen and Unplanned Pregnancy
1776 Massachusetts Ave. NW, Suite 200
Washington, DC 20036
phone: (202) 478-8500
fax: (202) 478-8588
e-mail: www.thenationalcampaign.org/contact-us/default.aspx
website: www.thenationalcampaign.org

The National Campaign to Prevent Teen and Unplanned Pregnancy promotes responsible behavior by teens and others regarding sexual matters and works to reduce the number of unplanned pregnancies each year in the United States.

National Institute for Reproductive Health

470 Park Ave. S., 7th Floor
New York, NY 10016
phone: (212) 343-2031
fax: (212) 343-0119
e-mail: info@nirhealth.org
website: www.nirhealth.org

The National Institute for Reproductive Health is committed to ensuring that all people have access to the highest-quality reproductive health care, including birth control—especially young women, low-income women, and women of color.

Planned Parenthood Federation of America

434 W. Thirty-Third St.
New York, NY 10001
phone: (212) 541-7800
fax: (212) 245-1845
website: www.plannedparenthood.org

Planned Parenthood promotes a common-sense approach to women's health and well-being based on respect for each individual's right to make informed, independent decisions about health, sex, and family planning, including using contraceptives to prevent pregnancy.

Scarleteen

e-mail: www.scarleteen.com/contact
website: www.scarleteen.com

Scarleteen is an independent, grassroots sexuality education and support organization and website. It is the highest-ranked website for sex education and sexuality advice online, including issues revolving around unplanned teen pregnancy and what to do about it.

Sexuality Information and Education Council of the United States (SIECUS)

90 John St., Suite 402
New York, NY 10038
phone: (212) 819-9770
fax: (212) 819-9776
e-mail: mrodriguez@siecus.org
website: www.siecus.org

SIECUS's primary goal is to provide the American public with education and information about sexuality and sexual and reproductive health, including school programs to educate students about how to avoid unintended pregnancy.

Additional Reading

Books

Douglas A. Abbot and Joseph M. White, *Flying High: Helping Teens Choose Abstinence*. Brigham City, UT: Brigham Distributing, 2011.

Jenny MacKay, *Teenage Pregnancy*. Farmington Hills, MI: Lucent, 2011.

Elizabeth Magill, *Pregnancy Information for Teens*. Detroit: Omnigraphics, 2012.

Hal Marcovitz, *How Should Sex Education Be Taught in Schools?* San Diego, CA: ReferencePoint, 2013.

Peggy J. Parks, *Teen Sex and Pregnancy*. San Diego, CA: ReferencePoint, 2012.

Jess C. Scott and Matt Posner, *Teen Guide to Sex and Relationships*. North Charleston, SC: Create Space, 2012.

Beverly Vincent and Robert Greenberger, *Frequently Asked Questions About Birth Control*. New York: Rosen Classroom, 2011.

Internet Sources

American Academy of Pediatrics, "Educating Your Teen About Birth Control," May 11, 2012. www.healthychildren.org/English/ages-stages/teen/dating-sex/Pages/Educating-Your-Teen-About-Birth-Control.aspx.

Mayo Clinic, "Birth Control Options: Things to Consider," January 27, 2012. www.mayoclinic.com/health/birth-control-options/MY01084.

NARAL Pro-Choice America, "School-Based Health Centers: A Vital Resource for Young People's Health," January 1, 2012. www.prochoiceamerica.org/media/fact-sheets/birth-control-school-health-centers.pdf.

Planned Parenthood Federation of America, "Info for Teens," 2012. www.plannedparenthood.org/info-for-teens.

Index

Note: Boldface page numbers indicate illustrations.

Picture Credits

About the Author

In addition to his many acclaimed volumes on ancient civilizations, historian Don Nardo has published several studies of modern scientific and medical discoveries and phenomena. They include *Force and Motion*, *Eating Disorders*, *The Scientific Revolution*, *Gravity*, *The Ice Ages*, *Germs*, *Cloning*, *Vaccines*, *DNA Forensics*, *Malnutrition*, and *Breast Cancer*. Nardo, who also composes orchestral music, lives with his wife, Christine, in Massachusetts.